T0183410

Lecture Notes in Artificial Intelligence   12025

Subseries of Lecture Notes in Computer Science

More information about this series at http://www.springer.com/series/1244

Mario Paolucci · Jaime Simão Sichman ·
Harko Verhagen (Eds.)

Multi-Agent-Based Simulation XX

20th International Workshop, MABS 2019
Montreal, QC, Canada, May 13, 2019
Revised Selected Papers

 Springer

Editors
Mario Paolucci (iD)
ISTC/CNR
Rome, Italy

Jaime Simão Sichman (iD)
Laboratório de Técnicas Inteligentes
Universidade de São Paulo
São Paulo, Brazil

Harko Verhagen (iD)
Institutionen för data- och systemvetenskap
Stockholm University
Kista, Sweden

ISSN 0302-9743 ISSN 1611-3349 (electronic)
Lecture Notes in Artificial Intelligence
ISBN 978-3-030-60842-2 ISBN 978-3-030-60843-9 (eBook)
https://doi.org/10.1007/978-3-030-60843-9

LNCS Sublibrary: SL7 – Artificial Intelligence

This Springer imprint is published by the registered company Springer Nature Switzerland AG
The registered company address is: Gewerbestrasse 11, 6330 Cham, Switzerland

Preface

This volume presents selected papers from the 20th International Workshop on Multi-Agent-Based Simulation (MABS 2019), a workshop hosted by the 18th International Conference on Autonomous Agents and Multi-Agent Systems (AAMAS 2019), which took place in Montreal, Canada, during May 13–17, 2019. The main scientific focus of MABS 2019, and of the present volume, lies in the confluence of social sciences and multi-agent systems, with a strong application/empirical vein. The workshop is concerned with (i) exploratory agent-based simulation as a principled way of undertaking scientific research in the social sciences and (ii) using social theories as an inspiration for new frameworks and developments in multi-agent systems.

The meeting of researchers from multi-agent systems (MAS) engineering and the social/economic/organizational sciences is recognized as a source of cross-fertilization, and it has undoubtedly contributed to the body of knowledge produced in the MAS area. The excellent quality level of this workshop has been recognized since its inception and its proceedings have been regularly published in Springer's *Lecture Notes in Artificial Intelligence* series. More information about the MABS workshop series may be found at https://www.pcs.usp.br/ ~ mabs/.

The goal of the workshop is to bring together researchers interested in MAS engineering with researchers aiming to find efficient solutions to model complex social systems from areas such as economics, management, organization science, and social sciences in general. In all these areas, agent theories, metaphors, models, analyses, experimental designs, empirical studies, and methodological principles all converge into simulation as a way of achieving explanations and predictions, exploration and testing of hypotheses, and better designs and systems.

We are very grateful to Jean-Daniel Kant, who gave a very inspiring invited talk on evaluation and design of policies, and to the participants who provided a lively atmosphere of debate during the presentation of the papers and during the general discussion about the challenges that the MABS field faces. We are also very grateful to all the members of the Program Committee and to external reviewers for their hard work.

In this edition, 15 submissions were received from which we selected 10 for presentation (near 66% acceptance) and 9 for the post-proceedings. The papers presented in the workshop have been revised and reviewed again in order to become part of this post-proceedings volume. The content of this volume can be divided in two main sections, the first containing policy-oriented models, and the second oriented to foundational models and models based on artefacts.

In the MABS and policy section, models are used to inform, plan, and support policy interventions. We have five papers in this section.

In "Modelling policy shift advocacy," Antoni Perello-Moragues, Pablo Noriega, Lucia Alexandra Popartan, and Manel Poch show how to create and study value-driven policy-making systems in the context of urban water management. The agents in the simulation can detect emergent phenomena and respond to them. This allows modeling of agents that are irrational, when goal satisfaction is unfeasible, misaligned between local and global policy spheres, and under the effect of policy-makers with limited competence.

Letícia da Silva Rodrigues, Sóstenes Gutembergue Mamedio Oliveira, Luiz Fernandez Lopez, and Jaime Simão Sichman present a simulation of the propagation of the Dengue virus in the second paper of this section, entilted "Agent based simulation of the Dengue virus propagation." The goal of the work was to compare its results with those that come from some traditional deterministic epidemiological models. Their simulation obtained the same macro behavior of the classical models, thus indicating that multi-agent models can represent reality at least as well as the classical models.

The third and fourth papers add to a fecund line of ABM research, the modeling of mobility, with both papers adding elements based on social and psychological aspects. In their paper, "On developing a more comprehensive decision-making architecture for empirical social research: agent-based simulation of mobility demands in Switzerland," Khoa Nguyen and René Schumann use a social psychology theory to frame modeling in an architecture aimed to improve communication between stakeholder and modelers. They apply a tree-like layered model for the generation of intentions and actions. Using this frame, they calibrate their model by matching answers from survey data to numeric simulation parameters. Juhi Singh, Atharva Deshpande, and Shrisha Rao use the boids model for motion, together with their own model of physical discomfort in "Modeling Pedestrian Behaviour Under Panic During a Fire Emergency." One of the potentially useful results of their approach is how clustering can slow down the evacuation process.

The fifth and last paper in this section, entitled "Reinforcement Learning of Supply Chain Control Policy using Closed Loop Multi Agent Simulation," models a supply chain including product unavailability, emptiness of shelves, product wastage, and over-supply. Souvik Barat, Harshad Khadilkar, Vinay Kulkarni, Vinita Baniwal, Hardik Meisheri, Monika Gajrani, and Prashant Kumar show how the reward function in a reinforcement learning model can be substituted with an agent-based simulation, adding elements such as uncertainty, adaptability, and emergent behavior, thus increasing the realism of the objective. This paper concludes the MABS and policy section.

The second section in the volume is related to MABS Foundations and Social Artifacts and includes four papers. In the first one, called "An Opinion Diffusion Model with Vigilant Agents and Deliberation," George Butler, Gabriella Pigozzi, and Juliette Rouchier extend the classic opinion dynamics model to include group-level deliberative discussions. The simulation results reveal that asking for more deliberation and including a larger percentage of agents in the deliberative instances (up to 25%, then the effect tapers off) guarantees better deliberated outcomes.

In the second paper, Samaneh Heidari, Nanda Wijermans, and Frank Dignum contribute to the debate on norms, reconnecting to the tradition that sees them as the embodiment of values. In "Agents with Dynamic Social Norms," the authors apply a value-driven norm specification that allows for explaining norm change in situations where agents can move between social groups.

The third paper, entitled "A collective action simulation platform" by Stephen Cranefield, Hannah Clark-Younger, and Geoff Hay, breaks the cage of simple game theory with agents that create explicit references to social expectations and manipulate them via a PROLOG-based module for event calculus. This is applied to a classic social dilemma, where it achieves social coordination instead of defection.

The last paper, whose authors are Samarth Swarup and Reza Rezazadegan, takes agents heterogeneity seriously, discussing it also as a simulation result and not only as simulation input. In fact, how good would it be to have heterogenous agents that all behave the same? In "Constructing an Agent Taxonomy from a Simulation through Topological Data Analysis," the authors take as an example evacuation simulation and show how their approach better detects group behavior, when compared with simple clustering. Moving to a more complex simulation of a disaster, they show how the topological approach allows extracting non-obvious taxa from the simulated behavior.

In order to conclude this brief review, and before leaving the reader with the content of the volume that we have roughly sketched in this introduction, we remark on the adoption of platforms and presentation standards in this year's papers. Of the nine papers, three of them did not name an agent software platform. Two of them used Repast, and one each used Netlogo, MASON, and the more recent, GAMA, respectively. The last paper used an actor-based platform named ESL. None of the papers mentioned the ODD standard in any of its implementations: for good or for bad, we are still in a multi-agent simulation babel tower.

April 2020   Mario Paolucci
                                                      Jaime Simão Sichman
                                                          Harko Verhagen

Organization

Chairs

Mario Paolucci	ISTC-CNR, Italy
Jaime Simão Sichman	University of São Paulo, Brazil
Harko Verhagen	Stockholm University, Sweden

Steering Committee

Frédéric Amblard	Toulouse 1 University Capitole, France
Luis Antunes	University of Lisbon, Portugal
Paul Davidsson	Malmö University, Sweden
Nigel Gilbert	University of Surrey, UK
Tim Gulden	George Mason University, USA
Emma Norling	The University of Sheffield, UK
Mario Paolucci	ISTC-CNR, Italy
Jaime Simão Sichman	University of São Paulo, Brazil
Takao Terano	Tokyo Institute of Technology, Japan

Program Committee

Diana Adamatti	Federal University of Rio Grande, Brazil
Frederic Amblard	Toulouse 1 University Capitole, France
Luis Antunes	University of Lisbon, Portugal
Tina Balke	Vanderlande Industries, The Netherlands
Joao Balsa	University of Lisbon, Portugal
Federico Bianchi	University of Bresica, Italy
Cristiano Castelfranchi	ISTC-CNR, Italy
Sung-Bae Cho	Yonsei University, South Korea
Paul Davidsson	Malmö University, Sweden
Frank Dignum	Utrecht University, The Netherlands
Graçaliz P. Dimuro	Federal University of Rio Grande, Brazil
Bruce Edmonds	Manchester Metropolitan University, UK
William Griffin	Arizona State University, USA
Francisco Grimaldo	Universitat de València, Spain
Laszlo Gulyas	AITIA International Informatics Inc., Hungary
Mirsad Hadzikadic	UNC Charlotte, USA
Rainer Hegselmann	University of Bayreuth, Germany
Marco Janssen	Arizona State University, USA
William Kennedy	George Mason University, USA
Ruth Meyer	Manchester Metropolitan University, UK
Jean-Pierre Muller	CIRAD, France

Luis Gustavo Nardin	National College of Ireland, Ireland
Emma Norling	The University of Sheffield, UK
Juan Pavón	Complutense University of Madrid, Spain
Mario Paolucci	ISTC-CNR, Italy
William Rand	University of Maryland, USA
Juliette Rouchier	LAMSADE, CNRS, France
Jaime Simão Sichman	University of São Paulo, Brazil
Samarth Swarup	University of Virginia, USA
Klaus Troitzsch	University of Koblenz, Germany
Natalie Van Der Wal	Vrije University Amsterdam, The Netherlands
Harko Verhagen	Stockholm University, Sweden
Neil Yorke-Smith	Delft University of Technology, The Netherlands

Additional Reviewers

Sergei Dytckov
Mahyar Tourchi Moghaddam

Contents

Constructing an Agent Taxonomy from a Simulation Through Topological Data Analysis

Samarth Swarup[(✉)] and Reza Rezazadegan

University of Virginia, Charlottesville, VA, USA
{swarup,rr7nz}@virginia.edu

Abstract. We investigate the use of topological data analysis (TDA) for automatically generating an agent taxonomy from the results of a multiagent simulation. This helps to simplify the results of a complex multiagent simulation and make it comprehensible in terms of the large-scale structure and emergent behavior induced by the dynamics of interaction in the simulation. We first do a toy evacuation simulation and show how TDA can be extended to apply to trajectory data. The results show that the extracted types of agents conform to the designed agent behavior and also to emergent structure due to agent interactions. We then apply the method to a sample of data from a large-scale disaster simulation and demonstrate the existence of multiple emergent types of agents.

Keywords: Topological data analysis · Simulation analytics · Agent taxonomy

1 Introduction

A common question that is raised, when a multiagent simulation is presented, is, "Do you have different types of agents?" Generally the intent of the question is with respect to the design of the simulation, i.e., whether the simulation has different types of agents by design. An example might be a disaster simulation that has civilians and emergency responders, or adults and children, etc. A typology by design helps to understand the structure of the simulation, since different types of agents might have different behaviors, which result in different types of trajectories through the state space of the simulation, and ultimately manifest in different outcomes.

However, the same question can be asked with respect to an analysis of the outputs of the simulation. In this case, the intent of the question is with respect to emergent behavior in the simulation. While there is still considerable debate about the definition of emergence, here we simply mean differences in agent behaviors that are not explicitly designed into the simulation, but are induced by the dynamics of interaction within the simulation.

© Springer Nature Switzerland AG 2020
M. Paolucci et al. (Eds.): MABS 2019, LNAI 12025, pp. 1–13, 2020.
https://doi.org/10.1007/978-3-030-60843-9_1

Constructing a typology of agents from the outputs of a simulation may, in a sense, be more instructive because *(1)* agents that are different by design may not exhibit significant differences in behavior during the actual running of the simulation, and *(2)* agents that are not different by design might still exhibit significant differences induced by the dynamics of interaction within the simulation. Thus the emergent typology offers insight into how the interaction dynamics drive the simulation to exhibit particular emergent outcomes, which can be more complex and subtle than the design of the simulation might suggest.

Our goal here is to devise a method for generating a *taxonomy* of agents from the results of a simulation. A taxonomy goes beyond a typology in that it not only identifies meaningful types from a data set, but also establishes relationships among those types. For example, a taxonomy of biological organisms generally groups them into "taxa" by shared morphological characteristics. It can also create a ranking by grouping the taxa, like a hierarchical clustering method.

Generating a taxonomy of agents in a multiagent simulation is useful not just for understanding the emergent structure of the simulation. It is also a very useful way to present the simulation to end-users. For example, operational end-users who actually have to implement response plans during a disaster recognize the existence of emergent roles and behavior [9,10], and would benefit greatly from this type of information. This would, in turn, allow progress towards using simulations in a prescriptive way [5], i.e., to use simulations to suggest operationalizable courses of action and response plans.

The rest of this paper is organized as follows. We begin by describing a toy simulation of an evacuation scenario. We analyze output agent spatial trajectories from this simulation and show that clustering alone is not sufficient to extract the different types of trajectories from the data. After that we describe the topological data analysis method with a simple example and show how we can extend it to trajectory analysis. We then apply TDA to the evacuation simulation data and show the resulting taxonomy of agents. To assess the method on a more complex data set, we use sample trajectory data that we obtained from a recent disaster simulation [8]. The result of applying TDA to this data set is considerably more complicated, but we show that a set of emergent categories of agents can still be extracted from the results. We end with a discussion of the method and possible extensions.

2   Evacuation Simulation

We created a simple simulation of an evacuation scenario, where we have a population moving over a road network and trying to reach some marked "exit" nodes. This is not meant to be a realistic evacuation simulation. It is a toy test-bed where we can design simple interactions between agents and observe their effects on the resulting agent spatio-temporal trajectories. This will help us evaluate the effectiveness of the TDA method for generating a taxonomy.

The main components of the simulation are 1. A population of agents, 2. A road network, and 3. A behavior model. We describe each of these next, as well as the format of the resulting outputs.

Population: The agent population is organized into groups of different sizes, from 1 to 4. Groups of size 1 are referred to as individuals, and the rest are referred to as group agents. Each agent is assigned an *age* and *gender*, though only the age is relevant to behavior, as we describe further below. Groups correspond to families and are assigned appropriate ages and genders. In particular, children (i.e., agents with age less than 18) are always group agents. A distribution over group sizes governs the relative numbers of individuals and group agents that are generated. In the experiments in this paper, we generated a population of 100 agents, of whom 50 were individuals and 50 were group agents. The latter were divided into 10 groups of size 2, 6 groups of size 3, and 3 groups of size 4.

Road Network: The evacuation is assumed to be taking place over a road network. We model this as a graph embedded in two dimensions. We construct the graph by generating a collection of random points in a square area and connecting each point to its k nearest neighbors. The points correspond to the nodes in the network and, thus, each node has a corresponding (x, y) location. The road network used in the simulations presented in the following sections is shown in Fig. 1. Two nodes were randomly selected as exit nodes. These are marked in green in Fig. 1. In our simple model, agents are assumed to be at the nodes (corresponding to intersections), and to move exactly one hop in a time step (if they choose to move at all). In the simulations used in this paper, we generated a road network with 100 nodes, where each node is connected to its four nearest neighbors.

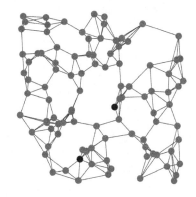

Fig. 1. Road network for the evacuation simulation. The exit nodes are marked in yellow. (Color figure online)

Behavior: We implement five different behaviors:

- **Evacuation**: This is the behavior where the agent is heading towards the closest exit node. This is implemented efficiently by using precomputed shortest paths from all nodes to the closest exit node. Individual agents always execute this behavior until they reach the exit node.
- **Rendezvous**: In this behavior, agents move towards their nearest group member. Once all the group members are at the same node, this behavior ends, and the entire group switches to the evacuation behavior.
- **Stay**: In this behavior, agents stay at their current node and do not move. This behavior is executed by all child agents until at least one of the adults from their group arrives at the same node. Thereafter child agents switch to rendezvous or evacuation, matching the collocated group members.
- **Exited**: Once an individual agent reaches an exit node, it has exited and so continues to be at that node for the rest of the simulation. Group agents

switch to the exited behavior only if the entire group is together when they reach the exit node. Otherwise, in the rendezvous behavior, they can pass through an exit node without switching to the exited behavior.

– **Do-nothing**: With a small probability, an agent in the evacuation or rendezvous behavior stays at its current node for one time step.

Simulation Outputs: Initially the agents are randomly distributed over the road network nodes. The simulation is then run for 20 time steps, which is sufficient for ~85 of the agents to reach the exit nodes. We output the spatio-temporal trajectories of all the agents as series of (x, y, t) tuples, where the (x, y) coordinates are the coordinates of the road network node the agent is at, at time step t, for $t \in [0, 20]$.

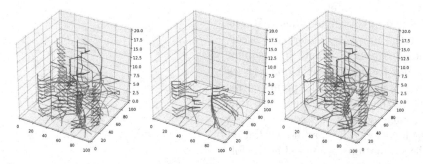

Fig. 2. Agent trajectories. The left panel shows the trajectories of all agents. When we split them into individuals and groups, we see that the trajectories of individuals (middle panel) look quite different from the trajectories of groups (right panel). The x and y axes show spatial locations. The z-axis is time. The colors are arbitrary.

The resulting trajectories are shown in Fig. 2. Though all the trajectories taken together are hard to parse visually, there is a hidden structure or typology induced by the dynamics, which is made clear when we separate out the individual and group agents.

The middle panel shows just the individual agents. Since these agents only do the evacuation and exited behaviors, these trajectories are qualitatively simple. They correspond to the shortest paths from the initial nodes of the agents to the closest exit nodes. Essentially, there are two types of agents here: those that go to one exit node, and those that go to the other exit node. This difference is entirely due to their initial location.

The right panel shows just the group agents, who have significantly more complicated trajectories. The rendezvous behavior results in trajectories that go away from the closest exit node, trajectories that have loops, and trajectories that show oscillations between two adjacent nodes. These last are due to group members ending up at adjacent nodes and then each trying to move to the other group members' location at each time step. The do-nothing behavior helps to escape this trap over time, but we see that in a couple of cases, the simulation hasn't run for long enough for the agents to stop oscillating.

3 Analysis by Clustering

We first analyze the set of trajectories by clustering, as follows. Paths in a graph G can be regarded as points in the high dimensional space of all the paths in G. As such a path is equivalent to a vector of adjacent vertices in the graph. To have a measure of similarity between paths, one can extend the graph distance into a distance between paths by using any of the L^p norms. This means if c, c' are two paths then we set $D_p(c, c') = \left(\sum d(c(i), c'(i))^p \right)^{1/p}$, where $c(i)$ refers to the ith element of c, and correspondingly for c'. The metric d can be the graph distance or, if the graph is embedded in Euclidean space, the Euclidean distance. Of particular interest are the cases $p = 2, \infty$. The latter gives us the maximum distance between the corresponding vertices of the graph.

To cluster the trajectories shown in Fig. 2, we used complete linkage clustering with the number of clusters set to either 2 or 4. In this method a dendrogram is obtained by recursively merging clusters of closest distance. The distance between two clusters is given by the maximum of distances between their elements. At the beginning each data point is a cluster of its own and at the end of the process all points are merged into one cluster. Given the desired number n of clusters, one uses the last level where there were n clusters in the dendrogram [6].

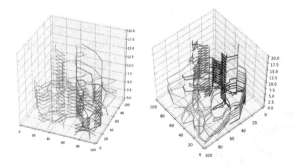

Fig. 3. Clustering the trajectories separates out the agents who go to one exit node vs. the other (green vs. blue), but does not separate the individual and group trajectories. (Color figure online)

The results of clustering are shown in Fig. 3. The left panel shows the results with number of clusters set to 2, and the right panel shows the results with the number of clusters set to 4. We see, in each case, that the nearby trajectories are grouped together, without distinction as to the structure or "complexity" of the trajectories. This is as expected, of course, but it demonstrates the inability of simple clustering to extract the real structure in the data, which is the distinction between the simple trajectories of individual agents and the complex trajectories of group agents. Thus, a taxonomy based on simple clustering would not give a meaningful set of categories of agents. Intuitively, the property we are trying to extract is captured by the shape of the trajectories, which suggests that a topological method might be better suited. So, we now turn to topological data analysis as a possible route to constructing a taxonomy. We first introduce TDA with a simple example, and then apply it to our simulation.

4   Topological Data Analysis (TDA)

Topology is the study of spaces equipped with a notion of neighborhood between their elements. Metric spaces (in particular graphs) are a particular example of topological spaces, though in general we do not need a metric to know which elements are neighbors. Other examples of topological spaces include simplicial complexes which are hypergraphs in which any subset of a hyper-edge is itself a hyper-edge. The dimension of a simplicial complex is the size of its largest hyper-edge minus one. In particular a graph is a simplicial complex of dimension one.

TDA aims to find a hypothetical topological space to which a given data set belongs. For example, we can take the proximity graph of a data set i.e., the graph obtained from the data set by connecting pairs of points whose distance is less than a given threshold. Once a topological space is associated to the data set, one can apply various topological methods and invariants to study the data and extract its inherent characteristics. As topology is the study of properties invariant under continuous transformations, TDA can be thought of as studying the properties of data which are robust w.r.t. continuous deformations of data. One prominent example of such an invariant is persistent homology [1] which has been applied to studying data in various different fields. However a precise description of persistent homology is beyond the scope of this paper.

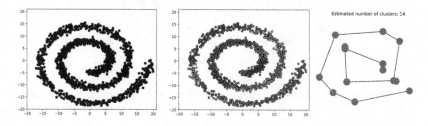

Fig. 4. Example of topological data analysis.

In a recent example, Lum et al. [4] use an enhanced method of clustering to assign a graph to the data. The data set is equipped with a filtration function and one uses this function to divide the dataset into a set of overlapping bins. One then clusters the data in each bin. Each such cluster gives us a vertex of the output graph and two such vertices are connected by an edge if their corresponding clusters have elements in common. This method is then applied to several data sets such as gene expression from breast tumors, voting data from the United States House of Representatives and player performance data from the NBA to obtain new insight on associations in among data points. In each case the authors find stratifications of the data which are more refined than those produced by traditional methods.

Figure 4 shows an example of TDA applied to a data set (left panel) which contains points along a spiral manifold. We used principal components analysis (PCA) to choose a direction for projection to a single dimension. The points were binned into five overlapping bins along this axis and the points in each bin were clustered in the original 2D space using DBSCAN [2]. The results of the clustering are shown in the middle panel. Each cluster was then replaced by a graph node placed at the cluster centroid (using Manhattan distance) and connected to neighboring nodes if the corresponding clusters shared any common points. This resulted in the graph structure shown in the panel on the right, which captures the essential spiral structure of the original data set.

Though it uses clustering, TDA is solving a fundamentally different problem. The spiral manifold data set doesn't have meaningful clusters. TDA is capturing the essential shape of the data set as a graph. The structure of the graph shows the linear structure of the data manifold. In addition, since the graph is embedded in two dimensions (each node has an (x, y) location derived from the data), it also captures the spiral structure of the manifold.

5 Analysis by TDA

To apply TDA to the study of agent trajectories, instead of using a filtration function as in [4], we can restrict the paths to possibly overlapping temporal regions. In this case we divide the runtime interval $[0, N]$ into intervals $[0, k], [k + 1, 2k], [2k + 1, 3k], \ldots$ and then cluster the restrictions of the paths to each subinterval as before. This way we obtain sets of clusters $C_0, C_1, \ldots C_n$ where $n = N/k$. We then connect with an edge the clusters in C_i and C_{i+1} that contain the restrictions of the same path.

An important special case is when $k = 0$. In this case the above procedure is equivalent to clustering the positions of the agents at each time step i and then connecting any cluster in C_i to those in C_{i+1} which contain the position of the same agent. This can be thought of as a coarsening of the trajectories.

In the other extreme, i.e., when $k = N$ we obtain the clustering of Sect. 3 back. Therefore we can regard our adaptation of TDA as a parametrized clustering method for agents.

Figure 5 shows the result of applying TDA to the agent trajectories. The graph has a somewhat complicated structure, so three different views are shown. The graph nodes corresponding to the exit nodes of the road network are marked. If all the trajectories assigned to a node are group agent trajectories, then the node is colored blue, otherwise it is colored gray.

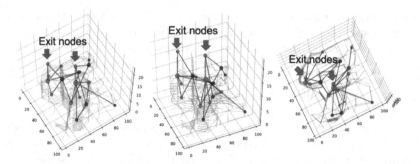

Fig. 5. Topological data analysis of agent trajectories. The three panels show three different views of the same graph, to help with understanding its 3D shape. The actual trajectories are shown in thin gray lines. We see that TDA is able to separate out several of the group trajectories, especially ones where the groups don't reach the exit. (Color figure online)

Taxonomy. We see that TDA is able to separate out several group trajectories, especially ones that don't reach the exit nodes. There are just two clusters (graph nodes) at the top level, five at the middle level, and ten at the bottom level. This gives us a nice taxonomy of the agents. Broadly, there are the two groups of agents that reach the two exit nodes. Even the agents that don't end up reaching one of the exit nodes are mapped to the closest exit node. Following the edges from the two top-level nodes gives us the five mid-level "taxa". Here the agents that don't reach the exit nodes are split off into their own categories. The lowest level taxa correspond to the early part of the simulation, and are therefore reflective of the starting locations of the agents.

We will now turn to a much more complex disaster simulation. We describe the simulation and the data set briefly first, and then present results from applying TDA.

6   Analysis of a Disaster Simulation

We obtained a sample of agent trajectories from a recent disaster simulation [8]. In this section, we briefly describe the simulation before going on to show the results of our method applied to the data set.

The scenario of the simulation is that an improvised nuclear device is detonated in Washington DC, USA. This hypothetical disaster is known as National Planning Scenario 1 (NPS-1) and has been studied extensively for many years We will refer to the simulation [8] as the NPS-1 simulation.

In the NPS-1 simulation, they modeled a detailed "synthetic" population of the region, including agent demographics, household structure, daily activity patterns, road networks, and various kinds of locations, such as workplaces, schools, government buildings, etc. This was a highly data-driven simulation, using data from multiple sources, such as the American Community Survey, the National Household Travel Survey, Navteq (road network data), Dun & Bradstreet (business location data), and more.

The simulation also contained models of multiple infrastructures, including power, communication, transportation, and health. Damage to these infrastructures affects the behavior and mobility of agents in the simulation in multiple ways. For instance, cell towers are inoperative close to ground zero, which means that people can't get in touch with family members, can't make 911 calls, and can't receive emergency broadcasts advising them to shelter in place. This lack of information affects agents' behavioral choices.

Similarly, damage to roads, as well as injuries and radiation sickness, prevent or limit agent mobility. Slow movement through areas close to ground zero also increases radiation exposure and exacerbates loss of health.

The simulation modeled six behaviors [8], as mentioned in Sect. 1. The behaviors were *household reconstitution, shelter-seeking, worry, evacuation, healthcare-seeking*, and *aiding & assisting*. These behaviors were implemented as specific policies, specified as short programs, over an action space that contained just two actions: moving (towards a destination) and calling (a family member, 911, etc.).

The simulation was run for 100 time steps. The first six time steps corresponded to 10 min intervals of real-time each, and the next 94 to 30 min of real-time each, giving a total of 48 h. We obtained a sample of 10,000 agents, out of a total of 730,833 agents modeled in the simulation. The variables included in the data set are *distance from ground zero* in meters, *level of radiation exposure* in centiGrays, *health state*, which is an integer in the range $[0, 7]$, and *behavior*, which is nominal, indicating which of the above behaviors an agent is executing at each time step.

6.1   Results

To enable viewing the results in a 3D plot as before, we restrict our analysis to pairs of variables (plus time). We also limit our TDA graph construction to time step 20 because we found that agent states don't change very much after that. To run TDA for the full sample of 10,000 agents takes a few hours (on a MacBook Pro with 2.6 GHz Intel Core i7 and 16 GB RAM), and results in a plot that is too cluttered to understand easily. Therefore, we demonstrate results with a random sample of 100 agents. We tried the analysis with multiple random samples of 100 agents, and the results are qualitatively similar each time.

Figures 6, 7, and 8 show the results. In each case the actual trajectories are shown with thin gray lines, while the TDA graph is shown in blue. The right panel of each of the figures shows a simplified version of the graph in the left panel, generated by homeomorphic smoothing (edge contraction) [3].

The idea of homeomorphic smoothing is to simplify a graph by removing nodes of degree 2 and connecting their neighbors to each other. The graphs generated by TDA often exhibit long paths where it follows a trajectory of an agent that doesn't interact with other agents. Examples can be seen on the left and right side of the left panel in Fig. 6.

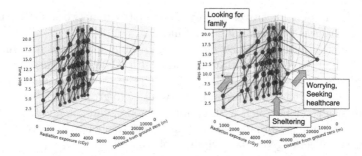

Fig. 6. Topological data analysis of 100 randomly chosen agent trajectories in the disaster simulation, where the variables are distance from ground zero and level of radiation exposure. The left panel shows the result of TDA, while the right panel shows the graph after homeomorphic smoothing (edge contraction). (Color figure online)

For the purpose of generating a taxonomy, these intermediate nodes in paths in the TDA graph don't add any information and can be removed. Depending on the structure of the graph, the impact of homeomorphic smoothing can be small (as in Fig. 6 and 7), or large (as in Fig. 8). Yet, though the right panel in Fig. 8 is greatly simplified compared to the left panel, it preserves the essential distinction between agents who have low radiation exposure and remain healthy vs agents whose radiation exposure increases over the course of the simulation, leading to a deterioration of their health condition.

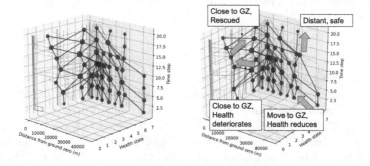

Fig. 7. Topological data analysis of 100 randomly chosen agent trajectories in the disaster simulation, where the variables are distance from ground zero and health state. The left panel shows the result of TDA, while the right panel shows the graph after homeomorphic smoothing (edge contraction). "GZ" is Ground Zero, i.e., the location where the bomb is detonated. (Color figure online)

Taxonomy. The annotations in Figs. 6, 7, and 8 show some of the taxa that emerge. In this case also, we can treat the graph nodes at the end of the simulation as the top level taxa in our emergent taxonomy. Thus, for example, in Fig. 7, the top level taxa correspond to agents who are

1. close to ground zero and in poor health,
2. close to ground zero and in good health,
3. at an intermediate distance from ground zero and in good health, and
4. far from ground zero and in good health.

As we follow the graph edges and move down from the top level, we can describe how the agents got to the states in the top level. These categories are annotated in the right panel of Fig. 7. Similarly, we can come up with descriptive categories of agents from the graph-based taxonomy in Figs. 6 and 8, as shown in the right panels of those figures. Thus the method gives us a ranked classification, i.e., a taxonomy, not just a typology of agents in the simulation. Importantly, these categories are not designed into the simulation, but emerge from the interactions induced by agent movement, communication, and behavior.

7 Discussion

The method presented here is a beginning to the solution of the problem posed in this paper. Topological data analysis, though an elegant idea, relies on clustering, which is still more of an art than a science. There is no doubt that the results presented here could be further improved through more experimentation. One possible direction for future research along these lines is to test the predictive power of the discovered taxonomy, e.g., can we use the taxa to predict the behavior the agents are engaged in? If that were to be the case, it would suggest applicability of this method beyond simulations, to predictive analysis of real-world disaster data.

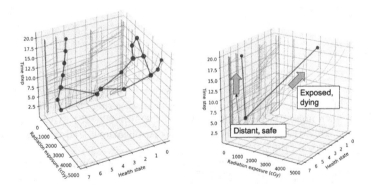

Fig. 8. Topological data analysis of 100 randomly chosen agent trajectories in the disaster simulation, where the variables are level of radiation exposure and health state. The left panel shows the result of TDA, while the right panel shows the graph after homeomorphic smoothing (edge contraction). (Color figure online)

The method presented also generalizes to higher dimensions, though we chose to stick to two dimensions (plus time) for our experiments for ease of presentation and understanding of the results. There is a need for a more rigorous method of evaluating the results from TDA in order to be able to use it well in higher dimensions. Presently, there isn't a good method for deciding how well the TDA graph captures the topology of the underlying data set. An important direction for future research is to connect TDA to more rigorously theoretical methods in topology like persistent homology.

Our experience here also suggests that, for complex simulations, the graph resulting from TDA might itself be too complex to understand. We further simplified it using homeomorphic smoothing, but other methods could possibly be developed for that. Other generalizations that are possible are to use tensor factorization to discover good filtrations when time is not one of the variables, and to develop a method for doing TDA on graphs when the graph is not embedded in Euclidean space. While distances are still well-defined in that case (shortest path distance), filtration and binning don't have obvious analogs.

More generally, we believe this is a helpful method for the broader goal of making simulations more usable and useful. Many simulation analytics methods are being developed which address different facets of simulation use, and these methods need to be brought together into a common framework. For example, the problem of simulation summarization [7] is clearly related to the problem of generating a taxonomy of agents. A user study could also be done to assess if operational users, such as emergency responders and planners, find this taxonomy useful or interesting. This would help improve the simulation as well as build trust in the methods on the part of the end-users, which is ultimately the biggest barrier to mainstream adoption of MAS methods.

Acknowledgments. S.S. was supported in part by DTRA CNIMS Contract HDTRA1-17-0118.

References

1. Carlsson, G.: Topology and data. Bull. Am. Math. Soc. **46**, 255–308 (2009)
2. Ester, M., Kriegel, H.P., Sander, J., Xu, X.: A density-based algorithm for discovering clusters a density-based algorithm for discovering clusters in large spatial databases with noise. In: Proceedings of the KDD, pp. 226–231. AAAI Press (1996)
3. Gross, J.L., Yellen, J.: Graph Theory and Its Applications, 2nd edn., p. 263. CRC Press, Boca Raton (1998)
4. Lum, P.Y., et al.: Extracting insights from the shape of complex data using topology. Sci. Rep. **3**, Article 1236 (2013)
5. Marathe, M., Mortveit, H., Parikh, N., Swarup, S.: Prescriptive analytics using synthetic information. In: Hsu, W.H. (ed.) Emerging Trends in Predictive Analytics: Risk Management and Decision Making, pp. 1–19. IGI Global, Hershey (2014)
6. Müllner, D.: fastcluster: fast hierarchical, agglomerative clustering routines for R and Python. J. Stat. Softw. **53**(9), 1–18 (2013)
7. Parikh, N., Marathe, M., Swarup, S.: Summarizing simulation results using causally-relevant states. In: Osman, N., Sierra, C. (eds.) AAMAS 2016. LNCS (LNAI), vol. 10003, pp. 88–103. Springer, Cham (2016). https://doi.org/10.1007/978-3-319-46840-2_6

8. Parikh, N., et al.: Modeling human behavior in the aftermath of a hypothetical improvised nuclear detonation. In: Proceedings of the AAMAS, Saint Paul, MN, USA, May 2013
9. Provitolo, D., Dubos-Paillard, E., Müller, J.P.: Emergent human behaviour during a disaster: thematic vs complex systems approaches. In: Proceedings of EPNACS 2011 within ECCS 2011, Vienna, Austria, 15 September 2011
10. Stallings, R.A., Quarantelli, E.L.: Emergent citizen groups and emergency management. Public Adm. Rev. **45**, 93–100 (1985). Special Issue: Emergency Management: A Challenge for Public Administration

Modeling Pedestrian Behavior Under Panic During a Fire Emergency

Juhi Singh$^{(\boxtimes)}$, Atharva Deshpande, and Shrisha Rao

International Institute of Information Technology, Bangalore, India
{juhi.singh,atharvaanant.deshpande}@iiitb.org, shrao@ieee.org

Abstract. This paper presents an integrated model that approximates pedestrian behavior in case of a fire emergency and its consequences. We have modeled a confined fire with a variable spread rate, based on the existing literature pertaining to the field. The fire has both psychological and physical impacts on the state of the agents. The model also incorporates clustering behavior in agents, which slows down the evacuation. The model helps recognize bottlenecks and compares the evacuation efficiency by comparing casualties across different scenarios. Simulation results are given as illustrations and give qualitative insights into the risks and likely problems in specific fire scenarios.

Keywords: Pedestrian evacuation · Compartment fire modeling · Clustering · Panic

1 Introduction

Large gatherings of people may need emergency evacuations due to sudden dangers. Unfortunately, such evacuations are quite difficult at the best of times, given the unpredictable nature of emergencies. Evacuations are even more complicated in case of fires, and such emergencies have caused mass casualties worldwide. For example, 117 people were killed in a fire at a garment factory in Bangladesh in 2012 [1]. A fire in a nightclub killed 100 people in Rhode Island in the US in 2003 [3], and the fire in the residential Grenfell Tower in the UK killed over 70 in June 2017 [12,13].

Since the conditions of such events are difficult to emulate, it is extremely difficult to obtain reliable data. This makes simulations indispensable for public safety. Agent-based modelling, in particular, has a role.

This work is based on the model by Trivedi and Rao [19] who use the Boids model [15]. Their model incorporates the effects of panic on decision making of agents, for instance increase in panic clouds the ability of the agents to make rational decisions [14]. The panic experienced by agents is quantified based upon its distance from the exit, the velocity of neighbors heading toward the exit, count of nearby agents who have high degrees of physical discomfort, and the lag in velocity compared to its neighbors, etc. [9]

© Springer Nature Switzerland AG 2020
M. Paolucci et al. (Eds.): MABS 2019, LNAI 12025, pp. 14–25, 2020.
https://doi.org/10.1007/978-3-030-60843-9_2

The social force model is used to calculate the force on an agent from its neighboring agents [5].

We have improved upon the existing framework, by further integrating real-life crowd behavior, using clustering [9]. We consider a group of evacuees as a network, with the agents as the nodes. Weighted edges between any two nodes represent the strength of a relationship or attachment between those particular nodes. Using this, we are able to model clustering behavior of pedestrians in our simulation, based upon the visibility, and the strength of attachment between any two (or more) nodes. Therefore, nodes with a high level of attachment tend to cluster together, instead of following the crowd path. This covers cases of families or friends clustering together, or people actively seeking out family members during emergency evacuations [5–7].

We further model a basic compartment fire, based on the fire model proposed by Bishop et al. [17]. We integrate the fire as a causative agent for the evacuation.

We use MASON, a Java-based multiagent simulation library, for our simulations.

2   Fire Model

We add a radially spreading, spherical fire as the hazardous factor in our simulations.

2.1   Background

We consider a compartment fire (one confined to a compartment) in our model. The lifetime of a compartment fire is characterized by the following stages [17]:

- Pre-Flashover Stage: This is the growth stage of the fire. The fire grows rapidly and is mostly fuel controlled.
- Flashover Stage: This is the stage of sharp increase in the hot gas temperature and fire intensity. This stage presents a non-linear stage of growth that leads to imminent disaster.
- Fully Developed Fire: This stage marks the fire reaching its maximum potential and engulfing the entire room.
- Decay Stage: This stage involves the period of decay of the fire, where the fire intensity gradually decreases.

We use a modified version of the fire model presented by Bishop et al. [17]. The model uses a zonal formalism for the modeling of fire. The compartment is divided into two zones: the hot gas layer and the rest of the compartment.

There is a constant exchange of heat that takes place between the fire, the hot gas layer and the walls of the compartment:

$$\frac{dE}{dt} = G(T,t) - L(T,t) \tag{1}$$

where, $G(T,t)$ is the gain in energy which is chiefly determined by the growth of the fire. $L(T,t)$ is the loss of energy through the walls and the vent/exit, T is the temperature any time t.

The existence of a feedback loop between the fire and the hot gas layer also affects the growth of the fire. The fire is responsible for an increase in the volume and temperature of the hot gas layer, which in turn radiates heat toward the base of the fire, causing an increase in the rate of growth of the fire. The fire's growth rate is positive at first, ultimately leveling off.

2.2 Modified Fire Model

We use the model and notations described by Bishop et al. [17]. The equation of the rate of change of temperature is derived from the energy equation of the hot gas layer:

$$\frac{dE}{dt} = G(T, R) - L(T, R) \tag{2}$$

where $G(T, R)$ and $L(T, R)$ represent the gain and loss in energy respectively, at radius R of fire, while T is the temperature of fire. We use the equation of rate of change of fire radius, also as given by Bishop et al. [17]:

$$\frac{dR}{dt} = V_f[1 - exp(\frac{R - R_{max}}{R_{edge}})] \tag{3}$$

where, V_f is the flame spread rate in m/s, R_{max} is the maximum radius and R_{edge} is the maximum distance over which the effect of the fuel is felt. We use a non-dimensional form (in reference to units) of the equation, presented above, to make them easier to deal with.

We use Takeda's expression [8] for the rate of flame spread in our model. It is dependent upon the air supply to the compartment. We assume a constant air supply, thus making the fire-spread rate independent of temperature excess and the non-dimensional radius. Therefore,

$$V_f = s_1 m_a \tag{4}$$

where, s_1 is the spread rate, $m_a = \frac{w\xi}{\sqrt{F_r}}$, where ξ is the ventilation parameter, w is the non-dimensional width of the exit and F_r is Froude number [17].

Also, temperature is assumed to be the "fast" variable that reaches a stage of quasi-stabilization quicker whereas radius is considered a "slow" variable. This makes the spread rate independent of the temperature [2,17].

Since maximum evacuation takes place during pre-flashover stage, we limit our simulation to it. We can vary two factors to achieve our goal, which being:

– Wall temperature parameter(u)
– Non-dimensional width of the exit.

We fix u to 0 which makes the walls perfectly conducting. This increases the loss in heat through the walls and makes heat loss a dominant factor, preventing flashover from taking place [17,18].

3   Agent Model

We use the model proposed by Trivedi and Rao [19], which makes use of the boids model [10] to govern the macro movements of the agents. The boids model allows us to model flock behavior using the following rules:

- Cohesion: individual agents (pedestrians) try to move towards the center of mass of the group.
- Separation: agents try to move away from neighboring agents that are too close i.e. that are within the ease distance.
- Alignment: agents try to align themselves with their neighboring agents.

We have also retained the model proposed by Trivedi and Rao [19] to calculate physical discomfort. The model uses the forces acting on the agent to determine the discomfort experienced by them. The following forces act on the agent in the existing model:

- contact force from other agents;
- forces from the surrounding walls; and
- force from obstacles (for obstacle avoidance).

We have incorporated clustering behavior in the existing model to account for real-life behavior observed in pedestrians in similar situations. Additionally, we have made changes to the existing model to incorporate the fire in the model. We introduce additional forces in our model to incorporate clustering and fire avoidance. The model makes use of changing priority orders based on the distance from the fire and the exit to calculate the forces acting on the agent.

3.1   Environment Description

The agents exist in an environment which is defined by the following set of properties [11, 22]:

- Accessible: The environment is accessible, since the agents have access to all the parameter values that are required by them to decide the course of action. This entails that we have allowed the agents access to parameters, such as their distance from the fire, direction to the exit door, the direction of the crowd movement, etc. Some additional parameters also become available to the agent depending upon its distance from additional exit doors, related agents etc.
- Non-Deterministic: The simulation model is non-deterministic. A multi-agent system is deterministic when any action in the environment has a guaranteed effect. However, incorporation of panic model, adds uncertainty to the decision making process of the agents.
- Dynamic: Our environment incorporates the fire model, which makes the environment dynamic. The fire adds an external factor that modifies the environment, irrespective of the actions of the agents.
- Continuous: Our environment allows an infinite number of actions and scenarios with each simulation, thus, making it continuous. Also, the model exists in continuous 2D space.

3.2 Additional Attributes and Behaviors

The agents themselves are defined by a 7-tuple $\langle r_i, w_i, b_i, p_i, v_i, l_i.\gamma_i \rangle$, [16,19] where the last attribute is the addition made by us to incorporate clustering.

- r_i: This is the radius associated with an agent.
- w_i: This is the weight of the agent.
- p_i: This is the position vector associated with the agent at any instance. This is used to determine the agent's position with respect to the exit as well as with the hazardous entity (in our case fire)
- v_i: This is the instantaneous velocity associated with the agent at any instance.
- l_i: This is the ease distance associated with an agent.
- γ_i: This is the panic associated with any agent at an instance of time.
- b_i: This is the number of "buddies" associated with any agent. Agents that are buddies, share some relationship, which influences their movements during the evacuation. For instance, family members share a buddy relationship.

There are radial distance associated with each agent that defines their range of response i.e. within these distances, the agent reacts to the impetus. They determine the region within which the agent exhibits cohesive, alignment behaviors (d_i^c and d_i^l respectively). d_i^a is the radial distance which determines the comfort zone of the agent. Therefore, it is the distance that agent a_i tries to maintain from any agent a_j, where $j \neq i$. We added two additional distances associated with each agent:

- d_i^v: This radial distance determines the region of visibility of agent a_i. Within d_i^v, the agent is visible to its buddies, for $b_i > 0$.
- d_i^f: This radial distance determines the region, within which, the presence of fire causes a sharp increase in the panic of the agent, along with a sudden increase in the velocity component in the direction opposite to the fire.

There are also "refinement factors" [19] associated with the agents. These refinement factors determine the influence, that each of the factors mentioned above, will have on the decision made by the agent at any instance of time. The five original multipliers used by Trivedi and Rao [19] are as follows:

- m_i^g: "Goal Multiplier"
- m_i^c: "Cohesion Multiplier"
- m_i^a: "Alignment Multiplier"
- m_i^s: "Separation Multiplier"—determines the factor associated with repulsive force between agents.
- m_i^o: "Obstacle Multiplier"—determines the factor associated with obstacle avoidance.

We add the following refinement factors to our model:

- m_i^f: Fire Multiplier: determines the intensity with which the agent avoids the fire. This takes precedence over the goal multiplier when the agent is within close proximity to the fire i.e. $p_{fire} - p_{agent} \leq d_i^f$.

- m_i^b: Buddy Multiplier: determines the factor of pursuit of related agents. This factor is non-zero only when the buddy agents are visible to our agent, i,e, when the number of buddies within $d_i^v \neq 0$. It also takes precedence over the Goal multiplier, but is always lesser than Fire Multiplier.

We use the panic model as proposed by Trivedi and Rao [19], wherein the panic experienced by the agents is quantified. The panic is dependent upon the distance from the exit, physical discomfort etc. [9]

We include an additional component of panic to account for the panic caused due tp proximity to fire:

$$p_5 = \frac{k}{(f_i - p_i)^2} \tag{5}$$

where, f_i is the center of the fire and K is any constant.

Thus, the modified equation for calculating panic is:

$$\zeta_t = \frac{1}{5} \sum_{k=1}^{5} P_k \tag{6}$$

where, ζ_t is the sum of all factors of panic at time t.

$$\gamma_{i,t} = (\gamma_{i,(t-1)} + \zeta_t)/2 \tag{7}$$

where, $\gamma_{i,t}$ is the panic level of ith agent at time $'t'$

3.3 Clustering Model

We create a network, wherein the agents belonging to the network correspond to nodes in the network, while edges between them denote a pre-existing relationship. The edges are weighted and their weights determine the strength of the relationship. For instance, close family ties have higher weights associated with their edges. The weights vary from 0 to 1 i.e. $0 < w_e \leq 1$. These weights determine the m_i^b associated with any relationship. In our model, we have randomly created this network, while putting a modifiable upper limit to the number and size of the clusters. This model's effect is dependent upon the visibility of the related agents. That is an agent starts moving towards a related agent, only when they become visible to them. The visibility range is given as follows:

$$d_i^v = c \cdot d_i^a \tag{8}$$

where c is a constant.

In the presence of visible related agents, our agent calculated the velocity vector through the following formula:

$$v_i^b = c \cdot m_i^b \tag{9}$$

where, c is any constant and

$$m_i^b = \begin{cases} k, & \text{if } n > 0 \\ 0, & \text{otherwise} \end{cases} \tag{10}$$

Where k is a constant $k \in R$. Also,

$$\begin{cases} k > m_i^g, & \text{if } w_e > T \\ k < m_i^g, & \text{otherwise} \end{cases} \tag{11}$$

where, n is the number of visible related agents and T is Threshold value.

Therefore, in cases where the relationship between agents is stronger than a certain threshold, reaching the related agent takes a higher priority than exiting. Instances of the above, have been found to frequently occur in real evacuation situations and are shown to slow down the evacuation process considerably.

Table 1. Properties of fire in simulation [17, 19]

Attribute	Symbol	Value
Length of the room (metres)	l_r	26
Maximum radius	m_f	$120/l_r$
Effect of radius	e_f	$80/l_r$
Spread rate	s_f	0.026
Width of ventilation	w_f	$1/l_r$
Ventilation factor	η	0.00792
Froude number	f_r	2.652

4   Integration of the Fire Model

We integrate the fire model, described above, in our simulation by adding the attribute r_c to fire: this refers to the radial distance within which the fire results in casualties of all the agents (all agents within this range are mortally injured).

As the agents reach within d_i^f distance of the fire, their goal changes from reaching the exit, to escaping the fire at any cost. This makes m_i^f the dominating refinement factor.

Proximity to the fire also increases the panic of the agent, thus kicking in self-preservative instincts and the agents try to create as much distance as possible from the fire.

The velocity, after fire integration, is calculated by Algorithm 1: In the algorithm, we make use of the function MOVE as defined by Trivedi and Rao [19].

5   Result

We simulate the model, in the following manner:

Algorithm 1. Goal Velocity Calculation

1: Calculate and assign velocity
2: $x_0, v_0 \leftarrow 0$
3: $x_0 \leftarrow p_e - p_i$
4: $v_0 \leftarrow \text{MOVE}(i)$ ▷ velocity component away from fire
5: **if** human within d_i^f **then**
6:     $x_1 \leftarrow (p_i - p_f)$
7: **end if**
8:   ▷ velocity component towards buddies
9: **for all** buddies of agent i **do**
10:      **if** buddy j within d_i^v **then**
11:          $x_2 \leftarrow x_2 + (p_j - p_i)$
12:      **end if**
13:      $x_2 \leftarrow x_2/(N_b - 1)$
14: **end for**   ▷ Velocity Calculation at time 't'
15: $v_t \leftarrow v_0 + x_1 \cdot m_i^f + x_2 \cdot m_i^b$
16: $v_t \leftarrow v_{t-1} \cdot \gamma_{i,t} + v_t \cdot (1 - \gamma_{i,t})$ ▷ Final velocity under the influence of panic

---

1. Create the environment. This involves setting up the room, deciding the number of agents, the position of the fire, etc.
2. Simulate fire, which requires the spread rate, etc., to be calculated.
3. Calculate refinement factors for each agent, depending upon its location and attributes.
4. Calculate panic which, along with the refinement factors, is required to estimate the final velocity.
5. Calculate the physical discomfort experienced by the agent.
6. Using the velocity calculations, update the location of the agent. The radius of the fire and its spread rate are also updated.

We consider different scenarios to demonstrate our results. All simulations are conducted using similar parameters in an effort to obtain better evaluations and comparisons. We do not claim that all the real scenarios are precisely described by these settings, but parameters are taken from prior sources to best replicate the real-world scenarios.

The properties of agents in simulation is taken from previous studies [5, 6, 19–21]. The properties of fire are taken from Bishop et al. [17] and scaled to fit our simulations. These are described in Table 1 [4, 17].

In these simulations, we aim to qualitatively analyze evacuation plans to get a better understanding of bottlenecks and critical paths formed during pedestrian evacuation.

The dimensions of the room and the initial environment are the same as the compartment size used by Trivedi and Rao [19]. We consider different sample cases by simulating singular vs dual exits in the room, and also by changing the location of the fire in the room. The cases are as follows:

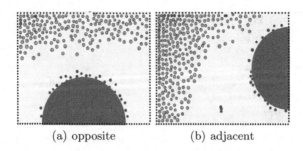

(a) opposite   (b) adjacent

Fig. 1. Case I with one exit door

Case I. *The position of fire with respect to the exit determines the number of casualties*: In this case, there is just one exit door for 400 agents. There are two sub-cases in these based on the position of fire in the compartment.
(a) Case I(a): The fire is positioned exactly on the opposite wall to exit door, as in Fig. 1(a)
(b) Case I(b): The fire is positioned in the middle of the one of the wall adjacent to the wall of the exit door as in Fig. 1(b)
We compared the casualties of these cases and observed that there was an increase of 12.048% in casualties from case $I(a)$ to $I(b)$. This is justified, since when the fire is opposite to the exit door, agents experience a repulsive force (due to the fire) in the direction of the goal (exit door). In the latter instance, the fire exerts a radial force, a component of which is in the direction opposite to the attractive force (toward the door).

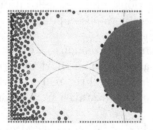

Fig. 2. Case II

Case II. *There is a decrease in casualties with multiple exits*: There are two exit doors in the middle of two opposite walls and fire is placed on the adjacent walls of exit doors as in Fig. 2. Both doors have equal visibility. There was a decrease of about 22.82% in casualties than in case $I(b)$ since there are two doors for exiting in case II even though the forces from fire act radially outwards and not toward the exit.
Case III. *The relative position of the gates in multi-exit determines the rate of evacuation*: In this case, there are two doors on the left wall instead of

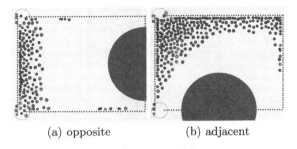

(a) opposite   (b) adjacent

Fig. 3. Case III

the middle. The circle around the exits represents the visibility of the doors. The cases are as follows:

(a) Case III(a): In this, the fire is opposite to the two exits, as shown in Fig. 3(a). In this case, the evacuation was faster and with fewer casualties.
(b) Case III(b): In this case, the fire position was adjacent to one of the exit doors, in Fig. 3(b). Here the evacuation was slower as one of the exit was too close to the fire and was thus inefficient as an exit door.
(c) Case III(c): In this case, there are two exits on the left but there is no fire. This case was taken as the base case for comparison.

Table 2. Comparison of evacuation times in Case III

Sub-cases	Evacuation time (seconds)
Case III (a)	34.86
Case III (b)	56.06
Case III (c)	48.31

The comparative analysis of these cases is shown in Table 2 (other cases can be compared similarly). We can see that, evacuation in case III(a) was observed to be faster than the case $III(c)$ as the repulsive force of fire acting on the agent aligns with the goal of exiting the door and thus it is faster than the case $III(c)$. In case III(b), the evacuation was slowest as one of the exits was too close to the fire and the agents were left with only one exit, at the corner, for evacuation.

We can also observe that placing exits at opposite corners, will be the most effective for evacuation, as at least one exit will remain fully functional in any case (i.e. any position of the fire)

Case IV. *Clustering slows down the rate of evacuation*: In this case, we have introduced clusters in case I(a)'s environment as shown in Fig. 4. The lines indicate the agents that are prone to clustering. Maximum number of clusters formed are 10 with the maximum number of agents being 6 in any cluster.

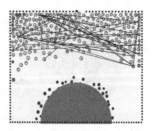

Fig. 4. Case IV

This was done in an effort to best replicate real world scenarios. Even with constraints such as visibility and random cluster sizes, clustering slowed down the evacuation process. We averaged out the time taken to evacuate over 20 samples, to account for the randomness in the cluster size and number. Evacuation time without clusters was 46.8 s. With the inclusion of clustering, the time increased by 27.9% and reached 59.9 s.

6   Conclusion

Our model improves upon the existing simulations of pedestrian behavior. We were able to show how clustering can slow down the evacuation process. There also seems to be a correlation between the position of the door with respect to potential fires and the evacuation process. We also looked at how the visibility and the number of doors affect the evacuation process. The use of our model is illustrated on a small set of scenarios. It can be applied to other cases, including realistic settings, by choosing parameters suitably.

References

1. Bajaj, V.: Fatal Fire in Bangladesh Highlights the Dangers Facing Garment Workers (2012). https://www.nytimes.com/2012/11/26/world/asia/bangladesh-fire-kills-more-than-100-and-injures-many.html
2. Drysdale, D.: An Introduction to Fire Dynamics. Wiley, Hoboken (1985)
3. Grosshandler, W.L., Bryner, N.P., Madrzykowski, D.M., Kuntz, K.: Report of the Technical Investigation of The Station Nightclub Fire (NIST NCSTAR 2), vol. 1. Technical report, National Institute of Standards and Technology (NIST), June 2005
4. Hägglund, B.: A room fire simulation model. Fire Mater. 8(2), 105–111. https://doi.org/10.1002/fam.810080208
5. Helbing, D., Farkas, I., Vicsek, T.: Simulating dynamical features of escape panic. Nature 407(6803), 487–490 (2000)
6. Helbing, D., Farkas, I.J., Molnar, P., Vicsek, T.: Simulation of pedestrian crowds in normal and evacuation situations. Pedestr. Evacuation Dyn. 21, 21–58 (2002)
7. Helbing, D., Johansson, A., Al-Abideen, H.Z.: Dynamics of crowd disasters: an empirical study. Phys. Rev. E 75(4), 046109 (2007)

8. Hisahiro Takeda, K.A.: New modeling of liquid or thermoplastic pool fires in compartment. In: Symposium (International) on Combustion, vol. 19, no. 1, pp. 897–904 (1982)

9. Lu, X., Luh, P., Tucker, A., Gifford, T., Astur, R.S., Olderman, N.: Impacts of anxiety in building fire and smoke evacuation: modeling and validation. IEEE Robot. Autom. Lett. 2(1), 255–260 (2017). https://doi.org/10.1109/LRA.2016.2579744

10. Luke, S., Cioffi-Revilla, C., Panait, L., Sullivan, K., Balan, G.: MASON: a multi-agent simulation environment. Simulation 81(7), 517–527 (2005)

11. Macal, C.M., North, M.J.: Tutorial on agent-based modelling and simulation. J. Simul. 4(3), 151–162 (2010). https://doi.org/10.1057/jos.2010.3

12. Moore-Bick, M.: Grenfell Tower Inquiry (2018). https://www.grenfelltowerinquiry.org.uk/

13. O'Hagan, A.: The tower. Lond. Rev. Books 40(11) (2018)

14. Pires, T.T.: An approach for modeling human cognitive behavior in evacuation models. Fire Saf. J. 40(2), 177–189 (2005)

15. Reynolds, C.W.: Flocks, herds and schools: a distributed behavioral model. In: ACM SIGGRAPH Computer Graphics, vol. 21, pp. 25–34. ACM (1987)

16. Rockenbach, G., Boeira, C., Schaffer, D., Antonitsch, A., Musse, S.: Simulating crowd evacuation: from comfort to panic situations, pp. 295–300 (11 2018). https://doi.org/10.1145/3267851.3267872

17. Bishop, S.R., Holborn, P.G., Beard, A.N., Drysdale, D.D.: Dynamic modelling of building fires. Appl. Math. Model. 17(4), 170–183 (1993). https://doi.org/10.1016/0307-904X(93)90105-P

18. Thomas, P., Bullen, M., Quintiere, J., McCaffrey, B.: Flashover and instabilities in fire behavior. Combust. Flame 38, 159–171 (1980). https://doi.org/10.1016/0010-2180(80)90048-6

19. Trivedi, A., Rao, S.: Agent-based modeling of emergency evacuations considering human panic behavior. IEEE Trans. Comput. Soc. Syst. 5(1), 277–288 (2018). https://doi.org/10.1109/TCSS.2017.2783332

20. Viswanathan, V., Lee, C.E., Lees, M.H., Cheong, S.A., Sloot, P.M.A.: Quantitative comparison between crowd models for evacuation planning and evaluation. Eur. Phys. J. B 87(2), 1–11 (2014). https://doi.org/10.1140/epjb/e2014-40699-x

21. Viswanathan, V., Lees, M.: An information processing based model of pre-evacuation behavior for agent based egress simulation. In: Weidmann, U., Kirsch, U., Schreckenberg, M. (eds.) Pedestrian and Evacuation Dynamics 2012, pp. 125–133. Springer, Cham (2014). https://doi.org/10.1007/978-3-319-02447-9_8

22. Wooldridge, M.: An Introduction to Multiagent Systems. Wiley, Hoboken (2002)

Reinforcement Learning of Supply Chain Control Policy Using Closed Loop Multi-agent Simulation

Souvik Barat[1]([✉])[iD], Prashant Kumar[1][iD], Monika Gajrani[1][iD],
Harshad Khadilkar[2][iD], Hardik Meisheri[2][iD], Vinita Baniwal[2][iD],
and Vinay Kulkarni[1][iD]

[1] TCS Research, Pune, India
souvik.barat@tcs.com
[2] TCS Research, Mumbai, India

Abstract. Reinforcement Learning (RL) has achieved a degree of success in control applications such as online gameplay and autonomous driving, but has rarely been used to manage operations of business-critical systems such as supply chains. A key aspect of using RL in the real world is to train the agent before deployment by computing the effect of its exploratory actions on the environment. While this effect is easy to compute for online gameplay (where the rules of the game are well known) and autonomous driving (where the dynamics of the vehicle are predictable), it is much more difficult for complex systems due to associated complexities, such as uncertainty, adaptability and emergent behaviour. In this paper, we describe a framework for effective integration of a reinforcement learning controller with an actor-based multi-agent simulation of the supply chain network including the warehouse, transportation system, and stores, with the objective of maximizing product availability while minimising wastage under constraints.

1 Introduction

Business-critical systems such as supply chain networks require continual evaluation and adjustment to stay competitive and economically viable in a dynamic environment. Reinforcement Learning (RL) [29,35] is a class of machine learning algorithms that can be used for controlling such complex systems in an adaptive and flexible manner. The goal of the system controller (also called *RL agent*) is to learn to take the best possible control actions in each possible state of the system, in order to maximise long-term system objectives. A crucial aspect of RL is the computation of next state and associated rewards for the chosen action(s), in a closed loop to enable learning. In compact systems with well-understood behaviour such as software-based games or vehicle dynamics, the action-driven state transition is simple to model, at least in terms of a probabilistic description. This is not the case for complex networked systems with a large number

© Springer Nature Switzerland AG 2020
M. Paolucci et al. (Eds.): MABS 2019, LNAI 12025, pp. 26–38, 2020.
https://doi.org/10.1007/978-3-030-60843-9_3

of entities that have their own micro-behaviour, and where the individual inter-actions build into emergent (and sometimes unpredictable) macro-behaviour. In such scenarios, top-down modelling allows for only a coarse approximation of the next states and rewards, hampering the training process of the RL agent.

A more accurate representation of the next state and reward (see Fig. 1), and con-sequently a better estimate of the long term consequences of a series of actions for an *exceedingly complex* [33] business-critical sys-tem such as a supply should be possible using a bottom-up multi-agent simulation approach. Fundamentally, these systems are *open* as they exchange messages with their

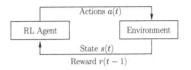

Fig. 1. Interaction of RL agent with an environment (actual system or simulation).

environment, and *complex* as they contain multiple non-linear feedback loops [3]. Moreover, these systems are not monolithic deterministic automatons, but are complex (scale-free) networks [5] or *systems of systems*, where the global behaviours emerge from the interactions of *autonomous*, *adaptable*, and *self-organising* sub-systems and constituent *agents* [15]. These characteristics pose obstacles to the application of alternative control approaches such as adaptive control and approximate dynamic programming. While the former requires an analytical representation of the control and adaptation laws, the latter requires at least a one-step rollout of a significant subset of actions, followed by a func-tional approximation of the subsequent value function.

We postulate that the use of analytical expressions for modelling (the method of choice for simpler RL applications [11,19]), is infeasible for complex systems, and instead advocate an agent/actor based modelling abstraction [1]. The paper presents a framework that uses reinforcement learning for exploring policies and deciding control actions, and an actor-based modelling and simulation technique to perform accurate long-term rollouts of the policies, in order to optimise the operation of complex systems. The key attraction of RL is that online deci-sion making is a one-shot forward pass through (typically) a set of neural net-works, and does not require online search. We use the domain of supply chain replenishment as an illustrative example to demonstrate the proposed modelling abstraction and its impact on training RL agent prior to its deployment.

2   Problem Formulation

Generic RL Problem: A reinforcement learning problem is described by a Markov Decision Process (MDP) [35] represented by a tuple $(\mathcal{S}, \mathcal{A}, \mathcal{R}, P, \gamma)$. Here, $\mathcal{S}$ is the set of states of the system, $\mathcal{A}$ is the set of control actions that the RL agent can choose from, $\mathcal{R}$ is the set of possible rewards, P is the (possibly stochastic) transition function from $\{\mathcal{S}, \mathcal{A}\} \to \mathcal{S}$, and γ is a discount factor for future rewards. In several cases, the agent is unable to observe the state space entirely, resulting in a partially-observable MDP or POMDP [35]. A set of observations $\mathcal{O}$ is derived from $\mathcal{S}$ to represent what the agent can sense. The goal of the RL agent is to compute a policy $\mathcal{O} \to \mathcal{A}$ that maximises the future discounted long-term reward. Clearly, an accurate representation of the transition function $P : \{\mathcal{O}, \mathcal{A}\} \to \mathcal{O}$ is a critical aspect of this effort.

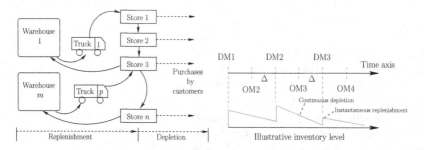

Fig. 2. [Left] Schematic of supply chain replenishment use case. [Right] Schematic of the periodic replenishment cycles. OM are ordering moments when the actions are computed, while DM are delivery moments when the inventory is actually delivered.

Specific Instance: We illustrate the generic RL problem in the context of supply chain replenishment, which presents well-known difficulties for effective control [22, 30]. The scenario is that of a grocery retailer with a network of stores and warehouses served by a fleet of trucks for transporting products. The goal of replenishment is to regulate the availability of the entire product range in each store, subject to the spatio-temporal constraints imposed by (i) available stocks in the warehouses, (ii) labour capacity for picking and packaging products in the warehouses, (iii) the volume and weight carrying capacity of the trucks, (iv) the transportation times between warehouses and stores, (v) the product receiving capacity of each store, and (vi) available shelf space for each product in each store. A schematic of the product flow is shown in Fig. 2 [Left].

A temporal illustration of the replenishment process is shown in Fig. 2 [Right]. The replenishment of inventory is assumed to take place periodically (typically every 6 h), at the time instants marked as DM (Delivery Moments). However, since it takes a non-zero amount of time to procure the new inventory within the warehouse, to transport it to the store, and to load it onto the shelves, the replenishment quantities of each product are computed at the time instants marked OM (Order Moments). There is a lead time Δ provided between each OM and the subsequent DM. The inventory of products is a monotonic non-increasing function between delivery moments, and there is a step increase at every DM when new inventory is provided to the stores.

Processes to be Modelled: The warehouses stock a range of products and supply them to the stores as described in Fig. 2. This involves packing the products (using trolleys), loading packed products to the trucks/carriers and delivering them to respective stores on predefined routes. Each sub-process contains constraints such as the warehouse labour capacity, machine capacity, number of trucks, and the truck volume/weight capacities. The uncertainties that emerge due to the probabilistic behaviours of the individual elements are: unavailability and varying productivity of the labours, sub-optimal machine throughput and unavailability and unaccounted delays of the trucks. Trucks are constrained by the volume and weight capacities, often they are suited for specific types of products and each of them has probabilistic characteristics, such as: propensity for transportation delay and break down.

Let us assume that there are m warehouses, p trucks, and n stores in the system. From operational perspective, each store stocks $i = \{1, \ldots, k\}$ unique varieties of products, each with a maximum shelf capacity $c_{i,j}$ where $j \leq n$ is the index of the store. Further, let us denote by $x_{i,j}(t)$ the inventory of product i in store j at time t. The replenishment quantities (*actions*) for delivery moment d are denoted by $a_{i,j}(t_d)$, and are to be computed at time $(t_d - \Delta)$. The observation $O(t_d - \Delta)$ consists of the inventory of each product in each store at the time, the demand forecast for each product between the next two delivery moments, and meta-data such as the unit volume v_i and weight w_i, and its shelf life l_i.

Note that the *states* differ from the *observations* in this case because the actual inventory at the time of replenishment is $x_{i,j}(t_d)$, which must be estimated based on the current inventory $x_{i,j}(t_d - \Delta)$ and some forecast of the depletion in the remaining time Δ. The inventory $x_{i,j}(t)$ depletes between two delivery moments $(d - 1)$ and d, and undergoes a step increase by amount $a_{i,j}(t_d)$ at time t_d. The actions are constrained by the various capacities in the system, including those within warehouses, in the transportation network, and in the store. The reward $r(t_{d-1})$ is a function of the previous actions $a_{i,j}(t_{d-1})$ and the evolution of inventory states $x_{i,j}(t)$ in $t \in [t_{d-1}, t_d)$. From a business perspective, of particular interest are: (i) the number of products that remain available throughout the time interval $[t_{d-1}, t_d)$, and (ii) the wastage of any products that remain unsold past their shelf lives. Mathematically, we define this as,

$$
r(t_{d-1}) = 1 - \frac{\text{count}(x_{i,j} < \rho)}{k\,n} - \frac{\sum_{i=1}^{k}\sum_{j=1}^{n} w_{i,j}(t_{d-1})}{\sum_{i=1}^{k}\sum_{j=1}^{n} X_{i,j}}, \tag{1}
$$

where $\text{count}(x_{i,j} < \rho)$ is the number of products that run out of inventory (drop below fraction ρ) at some time $t \in [t_{d-1}, t_d)$, $w_{i,j}(t_{d-1})$ is the number of units of product i in store j that had to be discarded in the time interval because they exceeded their shelf lives, and $X_{i,j}$ is the maximum shelf capacity for product i in store j. Since both negative terms in (1) fall in the range $[0, 1]$, we see that $-1 \leq r(t_{d-1}) \leq 1$. The goal of the control algorithm is to compute actions $a_{i,j}(t_{d-1})$ that maximise the discounted sum of these rewards from the present moment onwards, $\sum_{z=0}^{\infty} \gamma^z r(t_{d+z})$.

3   Related Work

Control Approaches: Supply chain control, including inventory management, has been a problem of interest for a long time [32]. Theoretically, such problems can be solved using mixed-integer linear programming [7,34], but this is infeasible at real-world scales. Instead, actual implementations typically use approximate methods such as threshold policies [9]. Other traditional methods such as state feedback [6] and model predictive control [24] have similar scaling issues. Adaptive critics [31] and reinforcement learning [12,17,27] have also been used in literature, but primarily for single-product scenarios. However, these methods along with approximate dynamic programming (ADP) are likely to be the best suited for our problem, because they are known to work in related areas.

ADP has been used for task allocation problems in transportation networks [13,37], but has the inherent restriction of requiring analytical descriptions of value functions and at least a one-step rollout of the policy. Imitation Learning has been used in robotics [10], but is only feasible where an expert policy is available to imitate. Reinforcement learning has been used in the computation of torque commands for robotic applications [20,28]. In these cases as well as other complex systems [11,19], the system models are analytically defined, thus simplifying the computation of step rewards and next state of the system. This is because RL is effective only when the (stochastic) transition functions closely approximate the real system to be controlled. In situations where the system cannot be described analytically, algebraic expressions cannot be used to compute rewards and transitions. Where RL has been used in supply chain management [12,17,27,38], it tends to focus on single-product scenarios. An experimental approach can be used for training the RL agent when the system is non-physical (for example, is itself a piece of software as in the case of computer games) [26]. However, applying experimental approach on the actual system is not feasible in the case of business-critical systems. Therefore, the development of (and integration with) a high-fidelity simulation model is crucial for effective training of the RL agent and controlling complex systems.

Modelling Approaches: Complex systems are typically modelled using two broad categories of approaches: *top-down* approach and *bottom-up* approach [36]. A *top-down* approach visualises a system from a higher scale and specifies aggregated macro-behaviour. This approach uses a range of models, such as *mathematical/analytical model* and *enterprise model* (EM), to represent and analyse the system as a whole. The *analytical models*, *e.g.*, Mixed Integer Linear Programming, represent a system using mathematical formulae and use rigorous mathematical and statistical problem solving techniques for system analysis. The *operational research techniques* are the specialised form of analytical models. The *enterprise models*, such as ArchiMate [16], BPMN [39] and System Dynamics [25], also serve a wide range of modelling and analysis needs by representing aggregated system behaviour. However, these approaches are found to be inadequate to represent systems (and their transition functions P) that contain multiple adaptable, self organising and uncertain entities (such as warehouses, trucks, products and store), individualistic behaviour (such as product expiry) and exhibit emergent behaviours (such as availability, unavailability and damages of products that are significantly influenced by several uncertain spatio-temporal aspects: transportation delay, inappropriate packaging with certain class of products, availability of other similar products, *etc.*).

The *bottom-up* approaches, such as *actor model of computation* [1] and multi-agent systems [23], capture the micro-behaviours of a system using a collection of interacting *actors* [1,14] or *agents* [23] (henceforth *actor*) and help to observe emergent macro-behaviour at a higher level of abstraction. The agent and actor based technologies, such as Erlang [4] and Akka [2], realise system as set of *autonomous, self-contained*, and *reactive actors*.

4   Solution Considerations and Proposed Approach

The proposed framework contains a RL agent based controller and two control loops as shown in Fig. 3. The model-based simulation loop helps to train RL agent and evaluate of new policies prior to their implementation in a real system, and real time control loop controls the real system using tranned RL agent. As shown in the figure, the controller

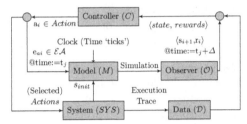

Fig. 3. Proposed approach.

decides an action based on its policy, *state* of the system and observed *rewards*. The model-based simulator consumes an action, which is produced by controller, as an external *event* and derives its impact by computing the *state* and *rewards* when a specific action is applied to the model. The model-based simulation loop iterates over multiple such actions to complete the necessary training. We adopt actor based simulation to specify the micro-behaviours of a system and compute emerging macro behaviours (*i.e.,* overall system *state* and *rewards*).

A meta-model to represent systems using an extended form of *actor* is shown in Fig. 4. Here, a system is a set of Actors, whose characteristics can be described using a set of variables or Properties. Each Actor has its own State and Behaviour. They interact with other Actors by consuming and producing Events, where an incoming (*i.e.* consumed) Event may trigger a Behaviour unit that can change the state of an Actor, send Events and create new Actors.

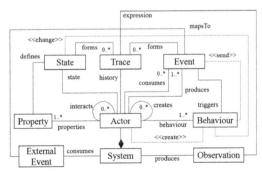

Fig. 4. Meta model to represent complex system using agents termed as 'actor'.

We extend this canonical form of an Actor with a notion of Trace (a sequence of information about State and Events) and an explicit construct to describe uncertainty in behavioural specification (as shown in Fig. 5). Formally, an actor (ACT) is a five-tuple: $\langle \mathcal{S}, \mathcal{EC}, \mathcal{EP}, Tr, \mathcal{B} \rangle$, where

```
1  stmt ::= become(state_new)        State change of an actor
2       | send(event_i, ACT_k)       Send event to an actor
3       | create ACT(state_init)     Create new actor
4       | e_1:stmt_1+...+e_n:stmt_n   Guarded statements
5       | probably(e_prop):stmt      Probabilistic statement
```

Fig. 5. Abstract syntax of behavioural statements.

S A set of labels that represent States of an Actor.

$\mathcal{EC}$ A finite set of Events that an Actor can consume.

$\mathcal{EP}$ A finite set of Events that an actor can produce. Here, $\mathcal{EC}$ and $\mathcal{EP}$ are not disjoint set (Events $\mathcal{EC} \cup \mathcal{EP}$ are consumed within an actor).

Tr A finite sequence of a tuple, where each tuple captures consumed Event, corresponding State and produced Event, $i.e.$, $s_0 \xrightarrow{ec0} \langle s_1, E_{ps1} \rangle \xrightarrow{ec1} \langle s_2, E_{ps2} \rangle ... \xrightarrow{ec(k-1)} \langle s_k, E_{pk} \rangle$, where $\{e_{c1},...,e_{c(k-1)}\} \in \mathcal{EC}$ and $E_{ps1},..., E_{pk} \subset \mathcal{EP}$

$\mathcal{B}$ A set of behavioural units. We consider that every behavioural unit $B \in \mathcal{B}$ is a set of programs that contain a sequence of stochastic statements. An abstract syntax to specify these programs is presented in Fig. 5.

In conformance with the meta model presented in Fig. 4, the system can be formally described as a quadruple $M = \langle \mathcal{ACT}, \mathcal{EA}, CLK, \mathcal{O} \rangle$, where $\mathcal{ACT}$ is a finite but dynamic set of actors; $\mathcal{EA}$ is a fixed and finite set of external Events, which are triggered from external sources; CLK is a clock that triggers virtual time Events or simulation 'ticks' (as external events) to progress simulation; and $\mathcal{O}$ is a set of observations. An observation is a tuple $\langle AS, Fact \rangle$, where AS is a set of actor states and $Fact$ are temporal expressions on actor traces ($e.g.$, occurrence of events over time). Two critical components of the control setup are described below.

Algorithm 1. Compute observations using Actor Simulation

```
 1: procedure SIMULATE(M_init, D, Δ)
 2:     Duration: D, observation interval: Δ, interval := 0, time := 0, state := Active
 3:     ∀ ACT_i ∈ ACT: create ACT_i(s_0)              ▷ Initiate simulation by instantiating actors
 4:     while (time != D) do                          ▷ Simulate for D time duration
 5:         receive(event_ext)                        ▷ M receives an external event
 6:         if (event_ext is 'tick') then             ▷ If event is a time event
 7:             time := time + 1
 8:             if (state := Active) then
 9:                 ∀ a_i∈ACT: send(event_ext,a_i)    ▷ Broadcast time event
10:             if (interval = Δ) then
11:                 interval := 0
12:                 O := observe(M)                   ▷ Compute O from all S and Tr of ACT
13:                 notify(O, C)                      ▷ Notify ⟨state_i,reward_i⟩ to C
14:                 state := Pause                    ▷ Pause time event for RL agent
15:             else
16:                 interval := interval + 1
17:         if (event_ext ∈ EA) then                  ▷ If event is a RL Agent action
18:             state := Active                       ▷ Restart time event for next observation
19:             for a_i ∈ ACT (of M) do
20:                 if (∃ e_x such that e_x ∈ EC of ACT_i And
21:                     map(e_ext,event_x) ∈ MAP) then
22:                     send(e_x,a_i)                 ▷ Send event to relevant actors
```

---

1. **Computation of** $\mathcal{O} \rightarrow \mathcal{A}$: The observations $\mathcal{O}$ consist of the inventories at time $(t - \Delta)$, the order forecast (expected depletion) $f_{i,j}$ in the next time period, and product meta-data v_i, w_i, and l_i. There are five input variables per product, leading to a total input size of $5kn$. The output size is kn, and each output can take any value between 0 and $X_{i,j}$. The number of variables in computing such a mapping directly using RL is infeasibly large. Therefore, we compute this mapping iteratively, one product at a time. We use a form of RL known as Advantage Actor Critic (A2C) [21] to compute the actions (not to be confused with 'actor' in the simulation context). The Actor is a neural network with 5 inputs and 11 outputs, representing discretised and normalised actions between 0 and 1. The Critic is a neural network with the same 5 inputs but a single output representing the expected *value* of the current observations. The basic reward function given in (1) was augmented for the purposes of training the agent, by a penalty on any actions that could not be feasibly implemented in the system because of capacity exceedance. This allows the RL agent to relate the effect of individual decisions on the net system reward.

2. **Computing** $\mathcal{A} \rightarrow \mathcal{O}$: The updates to $O \in \mathcal{O}$, the actor states, and events, are computed through simulation. As shown in Algorithm 1, all actors of an initial model (M_{init}) are instantiated to a random state or a system state to initialise a simulation. Actors execute their behaviours in their respective threads, interact with each other through actor events, change their states (possibly several times to respond to external and internal events) and create new actors. The external events that include time 'tick' and events corresponding to the RL actions are propagated to all relevant actors and allowed them to react for time duration Δ before the emergent states and traces are observed. The observed and computed O is then notified to the controller for the *next* RL action.

5   Illustration, Validation and Discussion

We use an actor language [8] that supports proposed actor abstraction to model a supply chain network as shown in Fig. 6. The simulation dashboard depicting the emerging reward related factors in a hypothetical retail chain is shown in Fig. 7. We use a data set spanning one year derived from a public source [18]. A total of 220 products were chosen from the data set, and their meta-data (not available originally) were defined manually. A single store and a single truck are used in the results presented here (see Sect. 6 for extensions). Forecasts were computed using a uniform 10-step trailing average for each product. The store capacity, truck volume and weight capacity, and labour counts were computed based on the order volumes seen in the data.

The time between successive delivery moments set to 6 h (leading to 4 DM per day). The lead time Δ was 3 h. The truck volume constraint was set lower than the average order numbers in order to stress the system. The initial normalised inventory level for each product is set to 0.5, and the level below which penalty is imposed is set to $\rho = 0.25$. Of the order data set, the first 225 days (900 DM) were used for training, while the remaining 124 days (496 delivery moments) were retained for testing. Figure 8 [Left] shows the training over 15 episodes,

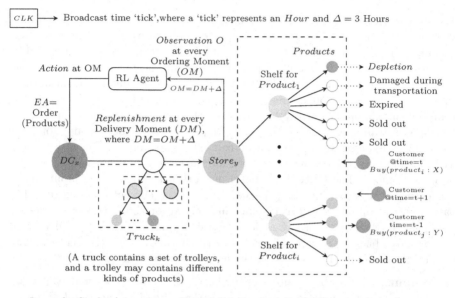

Legends: *Circle*: *Actor*, *Arrow*: Event interaction, and *Dotted Box*: containment
Observation O at OM_t:⟨ *Product Inventories* at OM_t, *Reward* from $OM_{(t-1)}$ to OM_t⟩
Reward: Function of products unavailability, expiry, and empty shelves

Fig. 6. An implementation of supply chain replenishment case study described in Fig. 2

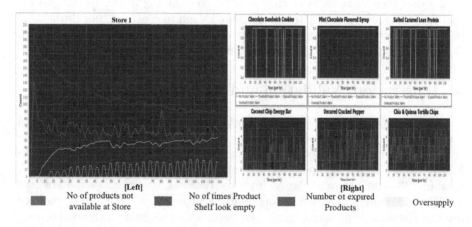

Fig. 7. [Left] Instance trace of product unavailability, emptiness of shelves, product wastage and product over-supply for a shop. [Right] Traces of individual products.

each spanning the 900 DM in the training data set. The average reward over all 220 products is seen to increase as training proceeds. The reward is compared with an industry-standard replenishment heuristic adapted from prior litera- ture [9]. We see that the reward at the end of training exceeds the heuristic performance, and this advantage is retained on the test data set as well (plotted using separate markers at the ends of the curves). Also shown in Fig. 8 [Left] is the 'exploration rate' of RL, which is the probability with which the RL algorithms takes randomised actions.

The performance advantage is due to the nature of Fig. 8 [Right], which plots the inventory levels of products on the test data set (496 delivery moments). Both algorithms begin with an initial (normalised) inventory level of 0.5 for all products. However, RL is able to maintain a higher average inventory level than the heuristic. The characteristics of the Critic and Actor networks of the RL agents are illustrated in Fig. 9. The value attached by the Critic network is shown in Fig. 9 [Left], as a function of the inventory level (after averaging over all other feature values). The peak value is near the penalty threshold $\rho = 0.25$. The value drops quickly below this level. There is also a decrease in the estimated value at very high inventory levels, due to the higher rates of product wastage. Figure 9 [Right] shows the replenishment quantity requested by the Actor network, again as a function of the inventory level of the product after averaging over all other features. We note that the requested replenishment rises as inventory levels drop from 0.5 towards the penalty threshold of 0.25.

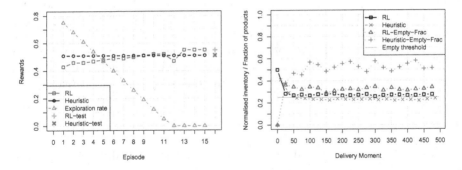

Fig. 8. [Left] Evolution of rewards during training, in comparison with the heuristic algorithm. [Right] Trend of average inventory levels across all 220 products over time.

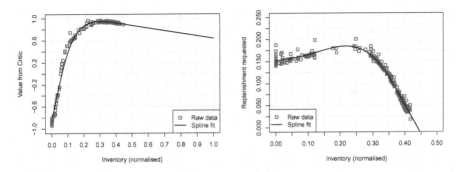

Fig. 9. [Left] Estimate of state value as a function of inventory. [Right] Replenishment requested by the RL agent as a function of current inventory level.

6 Conclusion

We described the use of a realistic closed loop multi-agent simulation model for training a reinforcement learning based control policy, as opposed to the traditional use of analytical expressions for rewards. Initial tests show that training using proposed approach is both feasible and effective. The use of the proposed actor based simulation as an environment to understand the overall implication of multiple RL actions (produced for different parts of a network) and locally optimised solutions for subsystems in a global system context, can also be viewed as a viable option. The ultimate goal of this work is to develop a closed-loop simulation and reinforcement learning framework, that allows us to deploy the trained agent on a real system with minimal subsequent adjustments.

A trained version of the reinforcement learning algorithm for computing replenishment orders is expected to become operational in a grocery retail network with approximately 10^3 stores and 10^5 products per store, in December 2019. The current setup has been tested on a single store scenario with nearly 10^4 products, which generates approximately 4×10^5 Actors in the simulation. The challenge in the coming year is to extend the capability to full system simulation while retaining computational feasibility. We believe this is feasible, based on the following considerations. First, the current implementation of the simulation and learning loop works on a single laptop. There is thus scope for increasing the computational power as necessary. Second, the decision-making portion ($\mathcal{O} \to \mathcal{A}$ map) works independently for each product, allowing us to parallelize the online workflow. Finally, it may be possible to loosely partition complex supply chain networks into sub-networks, further reducing the computational complexity.

References

1. Agha, G.A.: Actors: a model of concurrent computation in distributed systems. Technical report, DTIC Document (1985)
2. Allen, J.: Effective Akka. O'Reilly Media, Sebastopol (2013)
3. Anderson, P.: Perspective: complexity theory and organization science. Organ. Sci. **10**(3), 216–232 (1999)
4. Armstrong, J.: Erlang - a survey of the language and its industrial applications. In: Proceedings of the INAP, vol. 96 (1996)
5. Barabási, A.L., Bonabeau, E.: Scale-free networks. Sci. Am. **288**(5), 60–69 (2003)
6. Bouabdallah, S., Noth, A., Siegwart, R.: PID vs LQ control techniques applied to an indoor micro quadrotor. In: Proceedings of The IEEE International Conference on Intelligent Robots and Systems (IROS), pp. 2451–2456. IEEE (2004)
7. Caro, F., Gallien, J.: Inventory management of a fast-fashion retail network. Oper. Res. **58**(2), 257–273 (2010)
8. Clark, T., Kulkarni, V., Barat, S., Barn, B.: ESL: an actor-based platform for developing emergent behaviour organisation simulations. In: Demazeau, Y., Davidsson, P., Bajo, J., Vale, Z. (eds.) PAAMS 2017. LNCS (LNAI), vol. 10349, pp. 311–315. Springer, Cham (2017). https://doi.org/10.1007/978-3-319-59930-4_27
9. Condea, C., Thiesse, F., Fleisch, E.: RFID-enabled shelf replenishment with backroom monitoring in retail stores. Decis. Support Syst. **52**(4), 839–849 (2012)

10. Duan, Y., et al.: One-shot imitation learning. In: Proceedings of Conference on Neural Information Processing Systems (NIPS), vol. 31 (2017)

11. Gabel, T., Riedmiller, M.: Distributed policy search RL for job-shop scheduling tasks. Int. J. Prod. Res. **50**(1), 41–61 (2012)

12. Giannoccaro, I., Pontrandolfo, P.: Inventory management in supply chains: a reinforcement learning approach. Int. J. Prod. Econ. **78**(2), 153–161 (2002)

13. Godfrey, G.A., Powell, W.B.: An ADP algorithm for dynamic fleet management, I: single period travel times. Transp. Sci. **36**(1), 21–39 (2002)

14. Hewitt, C.: Actor model of computation: scalable robust information systems. arXiv preprint arXiv:1008.1459 (2010)

15. Holland, J.H.: Complex Adaptive Systems, pp. 17–30. Daedalus, Boston (1992)

16. Iacob, M., Jonkers, D.H., Lankhorst, M., Proper, E., Quartel, D.D.: Archimate 2.0 Specification. Van Haren Publishing, 's-Hertogenbosch (2012)

17. Jiang, C., Sheng, Z.: Case-based reinforcement learning for dynamic inventory control in a multi-agent supply-chain system. Expert Syst. Appl. **36**(3), 6520–6526 (2009)

18. Kaggle: Instacart market basket analysis data. https://www.kaggle.com/c/instacart-market-basket-analysis/data. Accessed August 2018

19. Khadilkar, H.: A scalable reinforcement learning algorithm for scheduling railway lines. IEEE Trans. ITS **20**, 727–736 (2018)

20. Kober, J., Bagnell, J.A., Peters, J.: Reinforcement learning in robotics: a survey. Int. J. Robot. Res. **32**(11), 1238–1274 (2013)

21. Konda, V.R., Tsitsiklis, J.N.: Actor-critic algorithms. In: Advances in Neural Information Processing Systems, pp. 1008–1014 (2000)

22. Lee, H.L., Padmanabhan, V., Whang, S.: Information distortion in a supply chain: The bullwhip effect. Manage. Sci. **43**(4), 546–558 (1997)

23. Macal, C.M., North, M.J.: Tutorial on agent-based modelling and simulation. J. Simul. **4**(3), 151–162 (2010)

24. Mayne, D.Q., Rawlings, J.B., Rao, C.V., Scokaert, P.O.: Constrained model predictive control: stability and optimality. Automatica **36**(6), 789–814 (2000)

25. Meadows, D.H., Wright, D.: Thinking in Systems. Chelsea Green Publishing, Hartford (2008)

26. Mnih, V., et al.: Playing Atari with deep reinforcement learning. arXiv preprint arXiv:1312.5602 (2013)

27. Mortazavi, A., Khamseh, A.A., Azimi, P.: Designing of an intelligent self-adaptive model for supply chain ordering management system. Eng. Appl. Artif. Intell. **37**, 207–220 (2015)

28. Powell, W.B.: AI, OR and control theory: a Rosetta stone for stochastic optimization. Princeton University (2012)

29. Russell, S.J., Norvig, P.: Artificial Intelligence: A Modern Approach. Pearson Education Limited, Kuala Lumpur (2016)

30. Sabri, E.H., Beamon, B.M.: A multi-objective approach to simultaneous strategic and operational planning in supply chain design. Omega **28**(5), 581–598 (2000)

31. Shervais, S., Shannon, T.T., Lendaris, G.G.: Intelligent supply chain management using adaptive critic learning. IEEE Trans. Syst. Man Cybern. Part A Syst. Hum. **33**(2), 235–244 (2003)

32. Silver, E.A.: Operations research in inventory management: a review and critique. Oper. Res. **29**(4), 628–645 (1981)

33. Simon, H.A.: The architecture of complexity. In: Facets of Systems Science, pp. 457–476. Springer, Boston (1991). https://doi.org/10.1007/978-1-4899-0718-9_31

34. Smith, S.A., Agrawal, N.: Management of multi-item retail inventory systems with demand substitution. Oper. Res. **48**(1), 50–64 (2000)
35. Sutton, R., Barto, A.: Reinforcement Learning, 2nd edn. MIT Press, Cambridge (2012)
36. Thomas, M., McGarry, F.: Top-down vs. bottom-up process improvement. IEEE Softw. **11**(4), 12–13 (1994)
37. Topaloglu, H., Powell, W.B.: Dynamic-programming approximations for stochastic time-staged integer multicommodity-flow problems. INFORMS J. Comput. **18**(1), 31–42 (2006)
38. Valluri, A., North, M.J., Macal, C.M.: Reinforcement learning in supply chains. Int. J. Neural Sys. **19**(05), 331–344 (2009)
39. White, S.A.: BPMN Modeling and Reference Guide (2008)

On Developing a More Comprehensive Decision-Making Architecture for Empirical Social Research: Agent-Based Simulation of Mobility Demands in Switzerland

Khoa Nguyen[✉] and René Schumann[✉]

HES-SO Valais Wallis, SiLab, Rue de Technpole 3, 3960 Sierre, Switzerland
{khoa.nguyen,rene.schumann}@hevs.ch
http://silab.hevs.ch

Abstract. Agent-based simulation is an alternative approach to traditional analytical methods for understanding and capturing different types of complex, dynamic interactive processes. However, the application of these models is currently not common in the field of socio-economical science and many researchers still consider them as intransparent, unreliable and unsuitable for prediction. One of the main reasons is that these models are often built on architectures derived from computational concepts, and hence do not speak to the selected domain's ontologies. Using Triandis' Theory of Interpersonal Behaviour, we are developing a new agent architecture for the choice model simulation that is capable of combining a diverse number of determinants in human decision-making and being enhanced by empirical data. It also aims to promote communication between technical scientists and other disciplines in a collaborative environment. This paper illustrates an overview of this architecture and its implementation in creating an agent population for the simulation of mobility demands in Switzerland.

Keywords: Agent architecture · Multi-agent system · Agent-based modelling · Discrete choice analysis

1 Introduction

The use of a specific architecture can facilitate the application of the agent-based methodology in a particular domain. Traditionally, economists tend to give importance to the selfish and rational part (*homo economicus*), while sociologists focus on the social capabilities (*Aristotle's zoon politikon*) and psychologists tend to see humans as mainly irrational and emotional. Thus, explicitly or not, agent-based models often follow one or another of these perspectives (e.g. [5,11,13]).

In recent years, we observe a trend of applying agent-based techniques to combine the views from different domains to provide more reliable descriptions

© Springer Nature Switzerland AG 2020
M. Paolucci et al. (Eds.): MABS 2019, LNAI 12025, pp. 39–54, 2020.
https://doi.org/10.1007/978-3-030-60843-9_4

for real-world phenomena [27] (e.g. self-organisation, the emergence of counter-intuitive behaviours [15]). This leads to the search for a generic computational platform that has a higher degree of abstraction, while can also be adapted as an illustration of a specific theory or hypothesis [8]. There is still, however, a lack of decision-making architecture that is expressive and flexible enough to build arguments both micro-macro levels in the socio-economical context [3,34].

This paper introduces an agent architecture for choice modelling simulation, which is inspired by Triandis' Theory of Interpersonal Behaviour (TIB) [38]. TIB states that behaviour is primarily a function of the intention to engage in the act, habit and facilitating conditions. It provides a meaningful set of determinants that contribute to decision-making in socio-psychology and can be used to produce statements about behaviours at society level as well as its members. Besides, the function given in TIB allows us to calculate the probability that a particular action will take place. By enhancing it with statistical data, this architecture can enable an agent-based model to have not only theoretical support from an established concept but also the capability to include empirical findings in scenario design. We demonstrate the implementation of this architecture in BedDeM (i.e. Behaviour-Driven Demand Model) - a simulation tool that aims to address both micro and macro perspectives of modal choice for mobility domain in Switzerland.

After considering some of the popular strategies for decision-making simulation in Sect. 2, a specification of the new architecture is presented (Sect. 3). Next, its contextualisation in the studied problem, Behavioural-driven Demand Model (BedDeM), is carried out in Sect. 4, especially focusing on the attribute definition, micro-behaviour and calibration. We then conclude our experience with the whole process and suggest further development in Sect. 5.

2   Related Works

For models that aim to understand the aggregate consequences of real-world phenomena, it is important to specify an agent's behaviours in a way that is both theoretically and empirically defensible [14]. There are different approaches for this issue in choice modelling, ranging from as basic as a reactive mechanism to the level of a complex entity using a cognitive model.

A simple design involves agents follow some sets of behaviour rules (i.e. decision-tree or production-rule systems), which apply both in the information-gathering stage and when making a final choice. It is typically used in conjunction with a set of assumed preferences for the agent to rank outcomes by desirability order. Examples include heuristics that update agent's behaviours according to the accumulated experience (e.g. [37]) or pick the next option that satisfies the qualities identified from empirical data analysis (e.g. [18]). In this setup, modellers have a straightforward job to trackback any changes in agents' behaviour but have to face a significant increase in computational complexity when a new rule is introduced [26].

Alternatively, researchers can choose to assign agents with beliefs, values or world views that correspond to observation from ethnographic data or stakeholder's assessment. A range of cognitive inspired agent architectures has been developed in recent years for this purpose. Mostly supported by process-based theories [34] and abounded rationality approach [31], they aim for providing a framework for a psychological mechanism through specifying essential structures, divisions of modules and their relations while always embodying fundamental theoretical assumptions [33]. One of the most well-known architecture is Belief-Desires-Intentions (BDI) [23]. It provides a robust standard framework for any agent-based simulation that wants to take into account human's decision-making process. However, these methods are often criticised for the lack of experimental grounding [7] and the agent choice of being homogeneous, completely rational and selfish [23].

Taking into account the dual nature of social processes, working on individual and societal levels requires the consideration of both and the interaction dynamics among them [10]. Thus, other cognitive models that add complexity to the classical rational agent, have emerged. Representatives for this category are CLARION [32], ACT-R [36], SOAR [19] etc. They usually take into account social theories and focus on different issues that were ignored in the rational agent. For example, Conte et al. [6] empower the social learning capabilities or Sun et al. [35] focus on organisational theories and the agent roles while others stress on the importance of beliefs in cognition [29]. There have been attempts in finding a global unifying principles for cognitive architecture (e.g. [7]), but it still remains an open debate [33,34]. Balke et al. [3] make a comparison between their features, which reveals none of the mentioned models is currently cover all socio-psychological aspects of decision-making (e.g. cognitive, affective, social, norm and learning).

Another popular approach is to enhance the agent's preferences, strategies and likelihood of making a particular decision with discrete choice models (e.g. [16]). Giving some defined set of possible options, it specifies a ranking order of these choice outcomes, which can then be converted into predicted probabilities. To produce an actual choice, a random component (representing human-error) can be introduced by sampling from a multinomial distribution with these probabilities. By incorporating empirical data (such as observed choices, survey responses to hypothetical scenarios or administrative records), the discrete choice model provides one flexible framework for estimating the parameter of choice behaviour, especially when there is a lack of information on which determinants affecting individual choice decisions. Despite that, without comprehensive support from a socio-psychological theory, current discrete choice models are often difficult for non-experts to understand the underlying implications of different modelling scenarios and associated behavioural assumptions [17].

3   Agent Architecture Design

3.1   Overview

An agent's main components and their functions are illustrated in Fig. 1. When a task is assigned, the *Perception* observes the current state of the environment, combines it with other's opinions and the agent's internal state to produce a list of available options. They are given to the *Decision-making* unit to be evaluated using the functions (or preferences) from the *Memory*. Details of this process are described in Sect. 3.2. The *Communication* component then utilises this result to output action to the environment. A social agent can have different agendas to archive (e.g. influence others' decisions and/or promote a certain action), which might affect the final outcome. There is an optional mechanism for the agent to remember the feedbacks from past actions for future decision-making cycles.

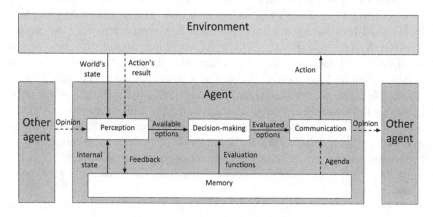

Fig. 1. Overview of agent's design

3.2   Decision-Making Procedure

Towards Human Psychology. To create a system that can mimic a human society, the first question to address is the origin of our behaviours. In psychology, different theories in the school of cognitive model describe this process, e.g. Ajzen and Fishbein's Theory of Reasoned Action (TRA) [9] and Ajzen's Theory of Planned Behaviour (TPB) [1], etc. They state that the key determinant of behaviour is an individual's intention to perform a specific act.

Triandis went beyond these theorists in his tri-level TIB model (see Fig. 2) by adding habits and facilitating conditions that either enable or hinder the performance of a particular behaviour. It stated that interpersonal behaviour is a multifaceted and complex phenomenon, due to the fact that in any interpersonal encounter, a person's action is determined by what that person perceives to be appropriate in that particular situation and by what others pressure them to do. The first level of TIB is concerned with the way personal characteristics and prior experiences shape personal attitudes, beliefs and social determinants related to the behaviour. The second level explains how cognition, affect and social determinants and personal normative beliefs influence the formation of intentions with regards to a specific behaviour. Finally, the third level states that intentions regarding the behaviour, prior experience and situational conditions predict whether or not the person will perform the behaviour in question.

We choose to implement TIB as it provides a comprehensive understanding as to what determines behaviour and is useful in explaining complex human thought processes, which are influenced by their social and physical environments. This would be valuable when presenting our platform to other discipline's scientists as our set of default parameters will come from Triandis' model. This set is also flexible enough to reflect other behaviour theories by exchanging psychology elements and assigning weights to mark their contribution to the agent's decision-making process.

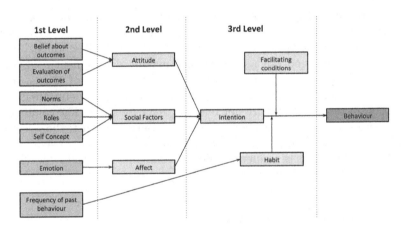

Fig. 2. Triandis' tri-level model [38]

Agent's Implementation. A full decision-making cycle with an example of a mobility application is illustrated in Fig. 3. An agent first selects an isolated decision-making task from the list that is sequentially executed. Its personal desire/goal is then combined with means provided by the external environment to generate a set of possible options. For all determinants (d), each option (opt) is given a referenced value which comes from comparing its property with other's ($R_d(opt)$). In the first level, this can be done using either a real numerical system (for determinants such as price or time) or ranking function (for determinants such as emotion). Both can be derived from empirical data (e.g. census/survey) or calibrated with expert's knowledge/stakeholder's assessment.

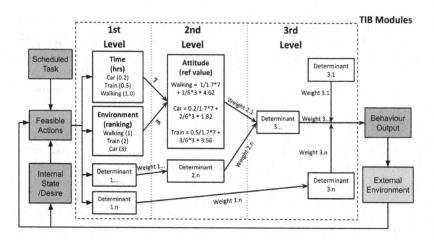

Fig. 3. Agent's decision-making procedure

The referenced values of these determinants are then normalised and multiplied with an associated weight (called w_d); the sum of which becomes the referenced value for the option in the next level (see Eq. 1). The weight, in this case, represents the importance of a decision-making determinant compare to others at the same level and emphasises on the heterogeneity of agents. It also allows the modeller to express a certain theory by cutting of determinants (by setting their values to 0) that are not relevant to a case study. The combination process then continues until it reaches the behaviour output list; the referenced value of which can be interpreted as the probabilities that an agent will perform that option. If the agent is assumed to be deterministic, it picks the option that is correlated to best-evaluated value.

$$R_d(opt) = \sum_{a=1}^{A}(R_a(opt)/(\sum_{o=1}^{O} R_a(o)) * w_a)$$

where
- $R_d(opt)$ is the reference value of an option (opt) at determinant d.
- A is the set of the ancestors of d (i.e. determinants connects with d in the previous level).
- O is the set of all available options.
- w_a is the weight of ancestor determinant (a).

(1)

In our mobility example (see Fig. 3), the agent has access to 3 options: *walking*, using *car* or taking *train*. In this study, we assume that smaller referenced value represent higher reference in the agent's decision. For a working trip of around 10 km distance, according to *time*, their referenced values are: $R_{time} =$ car (0.2), train (0.5), walking (1.0) (measured in hours); which combine to 1.7. According to *environmental friendly* determinant, they can be ranked as $R_{environment}$ = walking(1), train(2), car(3) (from best to worst); the sum of which is 6. If w_{time} and $w_{environment}$ are 7 and 3 respectively, the new referenced value in next level list($R_{attitude}$) of *walking* would be 1/1.7 * 7 + 1/6 * 3 ≈ 4.62, *car* would be 0.2/1.7 * 7 + 2/6 * 3 ≈ 1.82 and *train* would be 0.5/1.7 * 7 + 3/6 * 3 ≈ 3.56. Hence, according to *attitude, car* would have the highest chance to be picked for this individual agent, followed by *train* and *walking*.

4 A Mobility Simulation with the Behaviour-Driven Demand Model (BedDeM)

Our implementation platform - BedDeM - is being developed in Java using Repast library for agent-based modelling [24]. Its source code is currently available online at [4]. BedDeM's first application is in the mobility domain, which aims to generate yearly demands at the individual household level that can be interpreted at the granularity of a historical *evolution of transportation* for Switzerland. This mobility model is illustrated in Fig. 4. In this section, we first describe the technical details of the configuration of the agent population using statistical data. It is then followed by an overview of the simulation process and the calibration procedure.

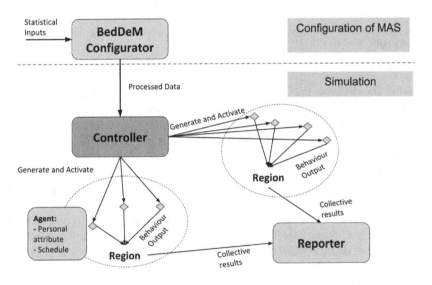

Fig. 4. Overview of BedDeM model

4.1 Agent Configuration

As mentioned in Sect. 3, the decision-making architecture requires two elements to calculate the probabilities for a set of options: (1) how to specify a ranking order of the option according to a determinant $(R_d(opt))$ and (2) the weight of the determinant (w_d). For this purpose, we utilise the Swiss Household Energy Demand Survey (SHEDS) [30]. There are several questions that compared the criteria for mobility mode choices, which answer can be interpreted as the weights(w_i) for different psychological determinants in TIB. A typical example can be observed from Fig. 5. A large number of similar questions can be categories into TIB determinants. However, as the first step into this experimental design, we decided on a mapping of a smaller set (see Table 1), which is based on some of the past researches [2] and what properties can be measured or ranked objectively (using common sense). Note that in this case, the determinant *belief* is omitted since the system assumes that the knowledge/perception of agents is always correct.

Please rate how important the following aspects are for choosing this mode of transportation.

	Not important 1 (1)	2 (2)	3 (3)	4 (4)	Extremely important 5 (5)
Choosing the cheapest option [_1]	O	O	O	O	O
I am used to taking this means of transport [_2]	O	O	O	O	O
Travelling as safely as possible [_3]	O	O	O	O	O
Travelling as fast as possible [_4]	O	O	O	O	O

Fig. 5. An example question from the Swiss Household Energy Demand Survey (SHEDS) [30]

Having the decision-making components figured, the next step is parametrising the profiles to build a synthetic population (see Fig. 6). This is accomplished by utilising another data source - the Mobility and Transport Microcensus (MTMC) [20], which includes the attributes listed in Table 2. Its entries (N = 57,091) are placed in a latent space (socio-matrix) that is represented by a symmetric Gower distance matrix [12]. All pairwise distances/dissimilarities are created based on the common features of the two data sources (e.g. age group, gender, region, household size, income level, number of personal vehicles). This matrix also provides a way to calculate the recommendation for agents from the same network (i.e. R_{role} - see Table 1). We then find the most similar peers that have the lowest distance towards each other and join them with entries from SHEDS (N = 5,515). A random number of representatives for each geographical region in Switzerland are selected to become our agent population (N = 3,080).

Along with the attributes in Table 2, a weekly schedule is also derived for each agent from MTMC to provide a way to calculate all relative costs for a trip (including purpose, distance, execution time). The agent's main purpose is to select a mode of transportation (including rail, car, bus, tram, biking, walking, others) to perform a task on its schedule. There is also an option of not performing the scheduled activity due to the constraints from the agent's states or environment (e.g. exhaustion of budget or exceeded travelling time on

Table 1. Mapping of TIB's determinants and SHEDS to initiate decision-making weights

Determinant	Layer	Measuring/Ranking property ($R(opt)$)	Matching question(s) in SHEDS (w, with scale 1 -5)
Evaluation - Price	1st	R_{price} = Cost of travelling	w_{price} = •Choosing the cheapest option
Evaluation - Time	1st	R_{time} = Duration of the trip (including the journey to station)	w_{time} = •Travelling as fast as possible
Norm - Environment Friendly	1st	R_{norm} = Motor type of the vehicle (Gas/Electric/No motor)	w_{norm} = •In the Swiss society, it is usually expected that one behaves in an environmentally friendly manner
Role - Environment Friendly	1st	R_{role} = Recommend from other agents in its network	w_{role} = •Most of my acquaintances expect that I behave in an environmentally friendly manner
Self-concept - Environment Friendly	1st	$R_{self-concept}$ = No data available - **to be calibrated** (see Sect. 4.3)	$w_{self-concept}$ = •I feel personally obliged to behave in an environmentally friendly manner as much as possible
Emotion - Enjoyment	1st	$R_{emotion}$ = Vehicle's comfortableness/luxury	$w_{emotion}$ = •I enjoy this way of travelling
Frequency of past behaviours	1st	R_{freq} = The number of usage over a certain period	w_{freq} = •I am used to taking this means of transport
Attitude	2nd	$R_{attitude} = R_{price}/\sum_{price} *w_{price} + R_{time}/\sum_{time} *w_{time}$	$w_{attitude}$ = •Wealth(material possessions,money)
Social factors	2nd	$R_{soc} = R_{norm}/\sum_{norm} *w_{norm} + R_{role}/\sum_{role} *w_{role} + R_{self}/\sum_{self} *w_{self}$	w_{soc} = Avg(•Equality •Social power •Authority •Protect the environment •Influential •Helpful •Prevent pollution)
Affect	2nd	$R_{affect} = R_{emotion} * w_{emotion}$	w_{soc} = Avg(•Pleasure •Enjoying life •Self-indulgent)
Facilitating conditions	3rd	R_{cond} = Does the trip pass all constrains? (e.g. time, budget, vehicle's availability) (0/1)	Agent filters the options that are possible to be performed that the time of decision-making
Habit	3rd	$R_{habit} = R_{freq} * w_{freq}$	w_{habit} = •Habit and Routine: I do without thinking
Intention	3rd	$R_{intent} = R_{attitude}/\sum_{attitude} *w_{attitude} + R_{soc}/\sum_{soc} *w_{soc} + R_{affect}/\sum_{affect} *w_{affect}$	w_{intent} = MAX_SCALE - •I do without thinking
Decision	Output	$R_{decision} = (R_{intent}/\sum_{intent} *w_{intent} + R_{habit}/\sum_{habit} *w_{habit}) * R_{cond}$	

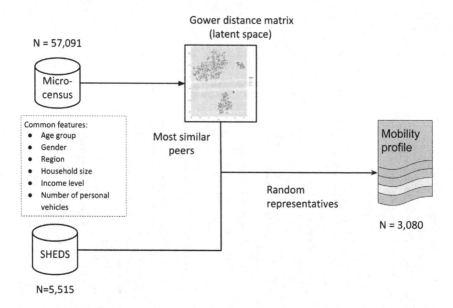

Fig. 6. Building a synthetic population

all available modes). Agents perform this filtering procedure before any decision-making activities (see determinant *Facilitating conditions* in Table 1).

4.2   Simulation Procedure

As shown in Fig. 4, the simulation process starts with a central controller creating all the agents with all their attributes and assigned them to their respective regions. Each region contains information about the available public transportations and can be used to reflect the dynamic change in traffic rate with regard to the simulating time. Initial values for these attributes are coming from the mapping process in Sect. 4.1. The agent then looks at its individual schedule and creates decision-making events to be activated. At the time of simulation, the controller triggers these events simultaneously, waits for them to finish, then skips to the next scheduled point (i.e. event-driven). At this developing stage, no learning technique is applied for feedback loops inside the agent's decision-making process. Agents simply keep track of the number of times its used a vehicle for trips of the same purpose, which is used for determinant *habit* (see Table 1). After all the tasks finished, a reporter component in the region collects the final results. Since each agent represents a portion of the total population, these numbers are then multiplied by the weight_to_universe parameter (see Table 2) to be compatible with MTMC for the calibration process.

4.3 Calibration

The purpose of calibration is to improve the compatibility of the current population with the target system (i.e. statistical data from MTMC). We are focusing on figuring out the most fitted ranking patterns for $R_{self-concept}$. Since the mapping question in SHEDS for this determinant is related to environmental friendly aspect of the option, we divided the agent population into 4 main profiles, depending on their daily main transportations: (1) soft-mobility modes (walking/biking), (2) public vehicles (tram/bus/train) (3) private vehicles (car/motorbike) and (4) others. $R_{self-concept}$ for each of them can then be calibrated by permuting the ranking order of all the modal choices.

Objective Function: Our main objective is to minimise the error calculated the Eq. 2. It is measured from the total differences between the final sum of kilometres in each mobility mode at the end of a period (i.e. a year in this case) and historical data. From MTMC [20], the total kilometres result for one year of all mobility profiles can be obtained (i.e. walking/biking, bus/tram/train, car/motorbike, others). Assuming that no two modes can be ranked in the same position, calibration involves using the permutation of these four sets of modes as configurations for the $R_{self-concept}$. We repeat this procedure for all agent's

Table 2. An agent's state attributes

Attribute	Brief description
Location	Region (or *Cantons* in Switzerland) in which the agent start its trips. It also provides information regard the availability of public transportations and local traffic rate
Budget	Weekly travelling budget
Accessibility set	List of available transportation services for the agent, which can be used to calculate all relative costs from a trip
Owned vehicles	List of vehicles that the agent own
Time and Distance to station	The average time and distance from the agent starting point to the closest station. They are used to calculate the evaluation of public modes
Discounts	List of discounts that applicable for the agent's trip
Weight to universe	The proportion of population that the agent represents

profiles set at either deterministic (choose the best option) or stochastic (choose from a random function with probabilities provided by sampling distribution of final referenced values) to find the smallest error.

$$\text{minimise} \atop conf \quad err(conf) = \sum_{i=1}^{M} |\, census_i - sim_i(conf)\,|$$

where
- $M = \{$walking/biking, bus/tram/train, car/motorbike, other$\}$.
- $conf = S(M) \oplus S(M) \oplus S(M) \oplus S(M)$, an instance of the concatenation of two permutation sequences of M.
- $census_i$ is census data for mode i (in kilometres).
- $sim_i(conf)$ is the simutation result for mode i (in kilometres).

$$(2)$$

Result: We list the kilometres in census data and the top results of two types of agents in Table 3. The best configuration is in the deterministic model with an error around 7.3×10^9 km, which accounts for 6.5% of the total scheduled kilometres. The main differences are in the *public* (i.e. walking/biking) numbers. We also observe that the stochastic error are much larger - above 51.8×10^9 km, which is only 46% accuracy. This is expected since agents in stochastic mode choose options based on a random function of probabilities derived from the referenced values. Currently, there is no pattern shown in the ranking function $R_{self-concept}$ of the results of *stochastic* mode, and hence additional runs with different distribution functions are needed in order to have a broader picture for this setting.

Table 3. Calibration results

Type	conf[a]	CM[b]	BTT[b]	WB[b]	O[b]	err[b]
Census		72.7	27.5	8.6	3.7	n/a
Deterministic	$R_{CM} = (1)$CM, (2)BTT, (3)WB, (4)O	73.1	26.7	3.3	4.4	7.3
	$R_{BTT} = (3)$CM, (1)BTT, (4)WB, (2)O					
	$R_{WB} = (4)$CM, (2)BTT, (1)WB, (3)O					
	$R_O = (2)$CM, (4)BTT, (3)WB, (1)O					
Stochastic	$R_{CM} = (1)$CM, (2)BTT, (4)WB, (3)O	46.7	6.0	5.0	4.6	51.9
	$R_{BTT} = (3)$CM, (1)BTT, (4)WB, (2)O					
	$R_{WB} = (4)$CM, (3)BTT, (1)WB, (2)O					
	$R_O = (4)$CM, (2)BTT, (3)WB, (1)O					

[a] Abbreviation - CM: Car/ Motobike, BTT: Bus/Tram/Train, WB: Walking/Biking, O:Others.
[b] All units are in 10^9 km.

5   Conclusion and Future Direction

The tree-like and layered structure of TIB has inspired us to develop a new agent architecture that can combine many different determinants in human decision-making; each of which can also be enhanced by empirical data. This has the potential to facilitate the uptake of socio-psychologists, economists and the general public with research projects. We demonstrate its practicality by creating a fully-working model to predict trends in the mobility domain for Switzerland - BedDeM. An agent population has been created and calibrated with the data of MTMC and SHEDS.

There is still some small margin error from the calibration process for deterministic setting (around 6.5% of the total scheduled kilometres). The agent's stochastic mode also does not reflect the macro patterns in MTMC effectively. Hence, we propose to address the issue of irrational behaviours by focusing on agent's learning in uncertainty environment (e.g. reacting to changes in traffic rate/break-downs and other's opinions) in the upcoming developing stage. Currently, agents are only keeping track of the number of times they used a mode on trips with the same purpose, which accounts for *habit* in decision-making (see Sect. 4.2). The influence of past experience to the ranking functions (i.e. feedback loops) can be further extended by modifying the agent's belief about the consequences or changing the weights of determinants to prioritise better alternatives. Studies in Reinforcement Learning techniques (e.g. [21]) or Generalized Expected Utility Theory (e.g. [22]) can be utilised for this purpose.

The next important step is assessing the model's variability and sensitivity. This can be done by selecting different representatives for the population when joining the two data sources. Although we have acquired the help of an economist specialised in environmental substantiality, it is also necessary to receive inputs from sociologist to derive alternative mappings of empirical data to TIB determinants (see Table 1) for more agent profiles. Further clustering technique on SHEDS panel data of the past few years would also give a good indication of how the weights of the determinants have changed, especially when there is an innovation in technology or policy-making. Coupling this with geographical statistics will allow us to observe how physical proximity, the layout of regions and other environmental elements can hinder or facilitate interaction and interdependence among social groups. Another potential research direction is comparing the efficiency of Triandis' Theory with other similar behavioural theories (e.g. Theory of Planned Behaviour [1]) by also changing the mapping of determinants. The next wave of microcensus (available in 2020) is a potential source for this test.

In term of validation, one of the good direction for our model is determining whether the key relationship or mechanisms highlighted in the agent-based model seem to be plausible explanations of real-world phenomena, which often involves analysis of empirical data that is separate from the agent-based model. Good data sources include other energy demand models in [28], which can be used to indicate the pattern in demand for the transportation sector. Another way to do this is to design an experimental scenario aimed at capturing mechanisms of interest. It can be done with the support of an expert in socio-psychology.

We close with a few words about software and documentation. As mentioned above, the core agent framework and BedDeM are developed in Java using an agent-based platform called RePast [24]. Although the current documentation is not comprehensive, its mechanism is easy to understand and has reduced the learning curve for the development process. RePast is also actively updated for newer Java version and functionalities. In addition, R language [25] is used to take care of handling and analysis to empirical input data. We have published the core architecture of BedDeM [4] and planned to provide further complex examples for the decision-making mechanism. This will allows us to have feedback from multiple perspectives in order to improve the platform so that it can be employed for researches across different domains.

Acknowledgement. This project is part of the activities of SCCER CREST, which is financially supported by the Swiss Commission for Technology and Innovation (Innosuisse). The current version also utilises data from the *Mobility and Transport Microcensus* - 2015 edition, which provided by the Federal Office for Spatial Development (ARE) in October 2017.

References

1. Ajzen, I.: The theory of planned behavior. Organ. Behav. Hum. Decis. Process. **50**(2), 179–211 (1991)
2. Ampt, E., et al.: Understanding voluntary travel behaviour change. Transp. Eng. Aust. **9**(2), 53 (2004)
3. Balke, T., Gilbert, N.: How do agents make decisions? A survey. J. Artif. Soc. Soc. Simul. **17**(4), 13 (2014)
4. BedDeM source code. https://github.com/SiLab-group/beddem_simulator. Accessed 12 Sept 2019
5. Bowles, S., Gintis, H.: Social preferences, homo economicus, and zoon politikon. In: The Oxford handbook of contextual political analysis, pp. 172–186. Oxford University Press, Oxford (2006)
6. Conte, R., Paolucci, M., et al.: Intelligent social learning. J. Artif. Soc. Soc. Simul. **4**(1), U61–U82 (2001)
7. Deffuant, G., Moss, S., Jager, W.: Dialogues concerning a (possibly) new science. J. Artif. Soc. Soc. Simul. **9**(1), 1 (2006). http://jasss.soc.surrey.ac.uk/9/1/1.html
8. Edmonds, B.: Simulation and complexity how they can relate. In; Virtual Worlds of Precision: Computer-Based Simulations in the Sciences and Social Sciences, pp. 5–32. Lit-Verlag, Münster (2005)
9. Fishbein, M., Ajzen, I., et al.: Intention and Behavior: An Introduction to Theory and Research. Addison-Wesley, Reading (1975)
10. Gilbert, N.: When does social simulation need cognitive models. Cognition and multi-agent interaction: From cognitive modeling to social simulation, pp. 428–432 (2006)
11. Gintis, H., et al.: Zoon Politikon: the evolutionary origins of human political systems. Curr. Anthropol. **56**(3), 340–341 (2015)
12. Gower, J.C.: A general coefficient of similarity and some of its properties. Biometrics **27**, 857–871 (1971)

13. Heckbert, S., Baynes, T., Reeson, A.: Agent-based modeling in ecological economics. Ann. N. Y. Acad. Sci. **1185**(1), 39–53 (2010)
14. Hedstrom, P.: Dissecting the Social: On the Principles of Analytical Sociology. Cambridge University Press, Cambridge (2005)
15. Helbing, D.: Systemic risks in society and economics. In: Helbing, D. (eds.) Social Self-Organization. Understanding Complex Systems, pp. 261–284. Springer, Heidelberg (2012). https://doi.org/10.1007/978-3-642-24004-1_14
16. Hörl, S., Balac, M., Axhausen, K.W.: A first look at bridging discrete choice modeling and agent-based microsimulation in MATSim. Procedia Comput. Sci. **130**, 900–907 (2018)
17. Keane, M.: Current issues in discrete choice modeling. Market. Lett. **8**(3), 307–322 (1997). https://doi.org/10.1023/A:1007912614003
18. Lady, B.B.F.: From pride and prejudice to persuasion satisficing in mate search. In: Simple Heuristics that make US Smart, p. 287 (1999)
19. Laird, J.E.: The Soar Cognitive Architecture. MIT Press, Cambridge (2012)
20. Mobility and Transport Microcensus. https://www.are.admin.ch/are/en/home/transport-and-infrastructure/data/mtmc.html. Accessed 16 Jan 2019
21. Mnih, V., et al.: Human-level control through deep reinforcement learning. Nature **518**(7540), 529 (2015)
22. Quiggin, J.: Generalized Expected Utility Theory: The Rank-dependent Model. Springer, Dordrecht (2012)
23. Rao, A.S., George, M.P.: Modeling rational agents within a BDI-architecture. In: Allen, J., Fikes, R., Sandewall, E., Sandewall, E. (eds.) Proceedings of the Second International Conference on Principles of Knowledge Representation and Reasoning, KR91. Morgan Kauffman, San Matteo, CA (1991)
24. The Repast Suite. https://repast.github.io. Accessed 24 Jan 2019
25. R project. https://www.r-project.org/about.html. Accessed 12 Sept 2019
26. Safavian, S.R., Landgrebe, D.: A survey of decision tree classifier methodology. IEEE Trans. Syst. Man Cybern. **21**(3), 660–674 (1991)
27. Sawyer, R.K.: Artificial societies: multiagent systems and the micro-macro link in sociological theory. Sociol. Methods Res. **31**(3), 325–363 (2003)
28. The SCCER-CEST Website. https://www.sccer-crest.ch/research-database/. Accessed 24 Jan 2019
29. Schill, K., Zetzsche, C., Hois, J.: A belief-based architecture for scene analysis: from sensorimotor features to knowledge and ontology. Fuzzy Sets Syst. **160**(10), 1507–1516 (2009)
30. Swiss Household Energy Demand Survey (SHEDS). https://www.sccer-crest.ch/research/swiss-household-energy-demand-survey-sheds/. Accessed 16 Jan 2019
31. Simon, H.A.: Bounded rationality. In: Eatwell J., Milgate M., Newman P. (eds.) Utility and Probability. The New Palgrave. Palgrave Macmillan, London, pp. 15–18. Springer (1990). https://doi.org/10.1007/978-1-349-20568-4_5
32. Sun, R.: The clarion cognitive architecture: extending cognitive modeling to social simulation. In: Cognition and Multi-agent Interaction, pp. 79–99 (2006)
33. Sun, R.: Cognition and multi-agent interaction: from cognitive modeling to social simulation. Cambridge University Press, Cambridge (2006)
34. Sun, R.: The Cambridge Handbook of Computational Psychology. Cambridge University Press, Cambridge (2008)
35. Sun, R., Naveh, I.: Simulating organizational decision-making using a cognitively realistic agent model. J. Artif. Soci. Soc. Simul. 7(3) (2004). http://jasss.soc.surrey.ac.uk/7/3/5.html

36. Taatgen, N.A., Lebiere, C., Anderson, J.R.: Modeling paradigms in ACT-R. In: Cognition and Multi-agent Interaction: From Cognitive Modeling To Social Simulation, pp. 29–52 (2006)
37. Todd, P.M., Billari, F.C., Simao, J.: Aggregate age-at-marriage patterns from individual mate-search heuristics. Demography **42**(3), 559–574 (2005). https://doi.org/10.1353/dem.2005.0027
38. Triandis, H.C.: Interpersonal Behavior. Brooks/Cole Pub, Co, California (1977)

Modelling Policy Shift Advocacy

Antoni Perello-Moragues[1,2,3]([✉]), Pablo Noriega[1], Lucia Alexandra Popartan[4], and Manel Poch[4]

[1] IIIA-CSIC, Barcelona, Spain
{tperello,pablo}@iiia.csic.es
[2] Aqualia, Madrid, Spain
[3] Universitat Autònoma de Barcelona, Barcelona, Spain
[4] LEQUIA, Universitat de Girona, Girona, Spain
{luciaalexandra.popartan,manuel.poch}@udg.edu

Abstract. In this paper, we propose to enrich standard agent-based social simulation for policy-making with affordances inspired by *second-order emergent social phenomena*. Namely, we explore the inclusion of agents who have means to perceive, aggregate and respond to emergent collective outcomes, for example by promoting some reaction in other agents. These enhancements are intended for a subclass of socio-cognitive technical systems that we call *value-driven policy-making systems*. We motivate and illustrate our proposal with a model of policy shift advocacy in urban water management.

Keywords: Agent-based social simulation · Socio-cognitive technical systems · Policy-making · Values · Second-order emergent phenomena · Socio-hydrology

1 Introduction

Agent-based social simulation (ABSS) has been shown to be an appropriate tool for policy-making [6]. Nonetheless, it has been suggested that in order to increase the usability for policy-making, standard ABSS may be enriched with some specific socio-cognitive *affordances* [12].

In this spirit, we proposed to afford some type of ethical reasoning and means to foster and assess moral behaviour [14]. The rationale being that, on the one hand, policy-makers draw on their political views and principles to design a policy intended to bring about a better state of the world, and deploy policy instruments that are consistent with such aim; and, on the other hand, those agents who are subject to such policy act according to their own values, interests and motivations [3,17].

With this understanding in mind, we characterised a type of agent-based simulators of public policies as a subclass of socio-cognitive technical systems [10], that we called *value-driven policy-making systems*. They involve *values* as a first class notion, and propose their operationalisation through *policy-schemas*, which consist of sets of *policy means* and *policy ends* [14].

© Springer Nature Switzerland AG 2020
M. Paolucci et al. (Eds.): MABS 2019, LNAI 12025, pp. 55–68, 2020.
https://doi.org/10.1007/978-3-030-60843-9_5

In this paper, we extend that work with an affordance that we find specially relevant in some policy domains; namely, means to perceive emergent collective outcomes and react by gathering social support for a response to that outcome. This affordance is inspired by the notion *second-order emergent social phenomena* [4,12]. To illustrate our proposal, we model the management of urban water and, more specifically, the interplay between influential stakeholders (e.g. political factions) and their target groups (households) in the process of advocating policy changes.

For these purposes, we start with a brief overview of our previous work and the type of second-order emergent social phenomena simulation we propose (Sect. 2). In Sect. 3 we propose the core components that extend our original conceptual framework for simulation of second order emergent phenomena. In Sect. 4 we outline a model for policy change advocacy in urban water management that shows how to instantiate the enhanced framework and discuss some simulation results. We close with remarks on further work (Sect. 5).

2   Background

1. Values. We assume a cognitive notion of value to model value-based reasoning for individuals, and value-based assessment of a state of the world [8,9,13,16,18]. Thus, we assume that values have the following properties [16]:

(P1): Values are beliefs;
(P2): Values refer to desirable goals;
(P3): Values serve as standards or criteria;
(P4): Values are ordered by importance;
(P5): The relative importance of multiple values guides action;
(P6): Values transcend specific situations.

In order to make these ideas operational (in a simulator), we assume a *consequentalist* view of values—values are known by their consequences and observable. In order to formulate assessments (and decisions) that involve several values we assume **commensurability**.

2. Socio-cognitive technical systems (SCTS) are situated, on-line, hybrid, open regulated multi-agent systems [10]. They are composed by two first class entities: a *social space* and participating *agents*, who have socio-cognitive (opaque) decision models that guide their actions. One may characterise subclasses of SCTS by postulating a meta-model that supports some specific affordances. Two remarks on this:

(i) The key idea is that an *instantiation* of a metamodel produces a formal or abstract *model* of a SCTS that belongs to that subclass [10] (see [2] for examples of metamodels).
(ii) An *affordance* is a property of the SCTS (of individual agents, of groups of agents or of social space) that supports effective interactions of agents within an SCTS. All SCTS require three affordances: (a) *Awareness*, which

provides participating entities access to those elements of the shared state of the world that should enable them to decide what to do; (b) *Coordination*, so that the actions of individuals are conducive to the collective endeavour that brings them to participate in the SCTS; and (c) *Validity*: the simulated world is a correct implementation of a model of the world, that is, the model is a faithful representation of the relevant part of the world and the simulated behaviour corresponds with the actual behaviour.

In a previous work [14], we proposed to model *value-driven policy-making systems* (*VDPMS*) as a sub-class of *SCTS* where values play a fundamental role in the regulation of the social space and in the decision-making of agents. We postulated a core meta-model whose main constructs are (Fig. 1):

(i) A **domain ontology** (like in any other SCTS) that establishes primitive entities that define the state of the world, actions and events that change that state. In simple terms, we assumed that policy-making occurs in a particular domain, that contains the relevant part of the world, within a social, environmental, economic context.

(ii) A **social model** containing at least two *agent roles*: (a) *policy-makers*, who aim at improving the state of the social space and institute means and ends in order to govern the activity of other agents; and (b) *policy-targets*, who are those that are affected by the policy, and whose behavioural change is going to drive the system towards that desirable state.

(iii) A (cyclic) **performative structure** involving a policy-design subprocess and other interrelated sub-processes like, negotiation, enactment, monitoring, assessment and revision.

(iv) The *policy-schema* data structure, composed of *means*—that aim to produce that behavioural change on policy-targets—and *ends*—that define those desirable world-states.

(v) A **policy schema** formed by a set of policy means (norms, incentives, actions, messages) and ends (goals that the policy means are meant to achieve).

(vi) A **value model**, consisting of a finite set of *values* ($\mathcal{V}$) and a *value profile* for each agent. A value profile includes a subset of $\mathcal{V}$ and a *value aggregation model* that the agent uses to assess the state of the world and make decisions. Values are projected onto the *policy-schema*, and *value aggregation models* are based on factual indicators.

3. Second order emergence social phenomena (*EP2*) refers to the idea that agents may recognise an emerging macro-phenomenon and, as a consequence, they intentionally react to it (support, change or contest) [4,12,15]. Castelfranchi [4] approached *EP2* as the *cognitive emergence* of the macro-phenomena in the agent's mind (i.e. recognition of the phenomena), and afterwards a process of *cognitive immergence* that changes its behaviour (i.e. consequential adaptation of the behaviour). He discusses examples where the awareness of the phenomenon can promote or discourage it, as, for instance, urban segregation: an agent, who wants to stay close to agents with similar cultural background, realises that the territory is becoming shared with agents with

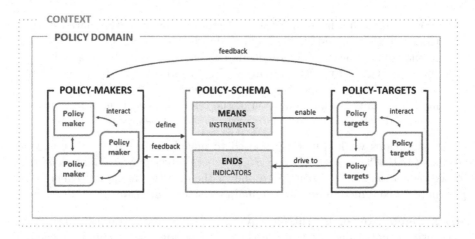

Fig. 1. Distinctive features of policy-making as a *value-driven socio-cognitive system* [14]

different cultural background, and as a consequence, its goal is to actively oppose new-coming residents in that territory.

In [12] it was discussed how to refine the class of SCTS in order to capture *EP2* features. In particular, *generic* affordances to support the simulation of *EP2* (in general), and affordances that are *specific* for a cognitive model of reputation.

3   An Enhanced Conceptual Framework for Modelling Policy Shift Advocacy

We want to enhance the core metamodel for value-driven policy-making systems (*VDPMS*), that we described in the previous section, with affordances for modelling some emergent second order social phenomena (*EP2*). More specifically, we want to model the processes through which some stakeholders seek support for initiatives that may affect the social space and specifically a current policy schema.

For instance in a *context* of a neighbourhood gentrification, an *influential* association of tenants may perceive a degradation of *conviviality* caused by an increase in the number of bars and the influx of tourism. The association *identifies* an "increase of police force" as a solution, and asks *households* to endorse it because it would increase *security*. If enough neighbours endorse the demand, the tenants association moves the proposal to the city government.

We propose to extend the core metamodel with the following elements:

(i) **EP2 perception**. That is, the generic affordances defined in [12] that enable an agent to perceive, assess and react to an emergent phenomenon.
(ii) **New actions:**
   (a) **formulate initiative**: broadcast an initiative to a group of policy-subjects

  (b) **process an initiative**: decide to endorse or not the demand, taking the appeal into consideration.
  (c) **support a demand**: express the endorsement of a demand
  (d) **move demand**: present a demand to a policy-maker
  (e) **enact demand**: modify the current policy-schema to accommodate the demand;
(iii) **New data structures**:
  (a) **Initiative** consists of a *demand* and an *appeal*
  (b) **Demand** is a change to the current policy-schema (actions, norms, incentives, campaigns)
  (c) **Appeal** a set of factual indicators and indexes, and an evaluation model.
(iv) **New roles**
  (a) **Policy-influencer**, who has EP2 perception and is capable to formulate initiatives and move and enact demands.
  (b) **Policy-target**, who is capable of evaluating an initiative and support a demand.

The key ideas are:

a. *Policy-influencers* are political stakeholders in the domain—with their own values and goals—and perceive and evaluate the world-state at the macro-level.
b. *Policy-targets* are not necessarily able to perceive emergent phenomena, but are capable of evaluating the state of the world at the macro-level since they have ethical and political interests.
c. *Policy-targets* may have no access to aggregated data but they may receive it, from *policy-influencers* and other sources, and then evaluate and react to it. *Influencer*'s opinion and information is more acceptable if it shares the values and the interests of the *policy-target* (i.e. the *policy-subject* is biased to consider the *policy-influencer* to be more trustworthy).

The rationale is that most citizens do not have enough resources (e.g. time, attention, motivation, economic, technical, etc.) to process and reason about data and information that concern macro-scales in multiple domains [1]. Nonetheless, citizens still participate in the political world. Usually, they retrieve information from trusted influential stakeholders that are capable of observing emergent macro-phenomena (e.g. gentrification, demographic change, water use trends, etc.). These *policy-influencers* are usually collectives (e.g. mass media companies, NGOs, think tanks, political parties, interest groups, social movements, etc.) that, if are displeased with the state of the world, may advocate for policy shifts, in order to imbue their values into public policies.

Agents use their *value aggregation models* to evaluate the state of the world and define their political satisfaction. Agents assess the current state of the world by comparing it with desired states. With this in mind, dissatisfaction with the current political situation may motivate political participation [11]. *Policy influencers* use their own value aggregation model to generate the appeals that are sent to *policy-target* agents, who then may support to produce policy

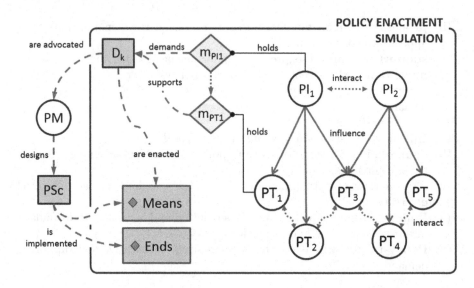

Fig. 2. Diagram of policy-influencers raising political demands for producing policy shifts as a consequence of the policy enactment

shifts. It is convenient to remark that *policy-targets* may perceive the world-state indirectly through *policy-influencers*.

Presumably, *policy-influencers' trustworthiness* and *relevance* arise from the citizen identifying with and sharing their values (at least, those that are publicised). Eventually, the citizen trusts the stakeholder, who shares the citizen's values and has its own political agenda, provides him with *useful* information and a *sound* framing (see [7]). This view is compatible with politics driven by group identities, which are not about adherence to a group ideology, but rather emotional attachments that transcend specific situations [1].

In crude terms, we implement *social support* and *policy shifts* as follows (Fig. 2):

1. The *policy-influencer* agent PI_1 has a political evaluation model m_{PI_1}, determined by a value aggregation model, that computes its political satisfaction.
2. The *policy-target* agent PT_1 "delegates" its model of political satisfaction to the *policy-influencer* PI_1. It receives m_{PI_1} and adapts its own model m_{PT_1} to take into account micro-level and macro-level features.
3. The *policy-target* agent PT_3 looks upon two *policy-influencers*, so it receives models m_{PI_1} and m_{PI_2}. It can take both for its own model m_{PT_3} (e.g. by combining them, discarding one, etc.).
4. If a *policy-influencer* is not politically satisfied (that is, the *desired world-state* and the *current world-state* are different enough), it may raise *political demands* D_k.
5. *Policy-targets* may support these, depending on their own satisfaction and values—if they are displeased, they will be open to interventions that change the world-state.

6. The *policy-maker* agent *PM* designs a *policy-schema PSc* (i.e. *means* and *ends*) according to its values and, presumably, taking into consideration the *political demands* raised in the social space.
7. It is possible that particular demands raised by *policy-influencers* may intervene directly on the social space bypassing *policy-makers* (e.g. persuading messages to encourage *policy-targets* to adopt social norms). This can be interpreted as new, enacted *means*.
8. Eventually, an updated *policy-schema* is enacted in the social space.

4   A Model of Policy Shift Advocacy

Picture a neighbourhood of a city: each household houses a family with a certain income level, water needs, and conservation practices. There is a water utility company that supplies water, a public service that is supported by a fee. Citizens assess the service they get and may at some point want to have better conditions. Their satisfaction depends on what they believe is important (i.e. values), and they may identify some ways of intervening politically in order to increase their level of satisfaction. However, this is based not only on those variables that affect them directly, but also on some features that affect the neighbourhood as a whole. Likewise, there are other stakeholders that assess the world-state with respect to their own values and may promote adjustments in the way water is being governed. As a consequence, there may be an interaction between stakeholders and citizens to stimulate political action, which implies multiple socio-cultural aspects around water governance (e.g. values, biases, trust, power, etc.). In this sense, households are often informed by public stakeholders, who may try to get support to their political demands by persuading households—yet their success would depend on the affinity with the values of the household.

Model. We model a crude urban environment to simulate the enactment of simplistic policies in a space formed by *policy-targets* and *policy-influencers* that hold different value profiles. The point of the exercise is to exemplify the affordances to explore social support of public policies and potential policy shifts, and to illustrate the interplay between *policy-targets* (i.e. households) and *policy-influencers* (i.e. public influencers). This specification of the meta-model featuring policy shifts is summarised in Table 1.

The model represents an urban region and it is focused on the water supply public service and how its policies affect the world-state. On the one hand, citizens make use of the water supply for their basic needs, but they want the service to be managed according to their understanding of justice and welfare as well. On the other hand, influential stakeholders may raise political demands if they consider that the world-state is not aligned with their public values.

Agents. We consider two type of agents in the artificial society: (a) *households* (i.e. *policy-targets*) and (b) *public influencers* (i.e. *policy-influencers*). *Households* are characterised by (i) value profile; (ii) number of members; (iii) income;(iv) water use;(v) conservation practices;(vi) service satisfaction; and

Table 1. Specification of the meta-model in a simple computational model

Network	Demand	Set by	Supported by	Type
	Suppress social aid	PI1	E-C, E-O	Advocacy
	Establish social aid	PI2	T-C, T-O	Advocacy
	Change management	PI1, PI2	E-O, T-O	Advocacy
	Control water use	PI1, PI2	E-C, T-C	Enacted

Table 2. Actions of households depending on the environment of intervention

Local	Political
Use water	
Adopt water conservation practices	Retrieve information
Perceive/Evaluate service	Support demands
Global assessment	

(vii) political satisfaction. Elements (ii–iii) are based on real-data (from the Spanish Statistical Office), (iv–vii) evolve as results of the simulation, and (i) is an input of the model. *Public influencers* are characterised by (i) value profile; and (ii) political satisfaction.

Scales and Process Overview. The model simulates one decade of activity through discrete time steps of one month. Each month households use water and pay the water fees, may adopt conservation practices, assess their satisfaction, and may support political demands (Table 2). Likewise, public influencers evaluate the world-state and may raise political demands (Table 3). Pre-conditions and post-conditions of these actions may depend on the values held by agents (for instance, a household may adopt conservation practices to protect the environment, while another may do so to have more wealth to spend in other goods). Spatially, the model represents an urban district.

Value Profiles. Public influencers hold *public values*, that concern the public affairs of the neighbourhood as a whole, for which we use the work on Public Service Values [18]. Households hold *motivational values*, related to needs and goals, for which we use the Schwartz Theory of Basic Values [16], and it is recognised that they also hold *public values*, which are defined by their interaction with the public influencers. In other words, households' values play a role in defining their satisfaction model with regard to the water service at home and

Table 3. Actions of public influencers depending on the environment of intervention

Local	Political
–	Perceive/Evaluate world-state
	Advocate/Enact demands
	Withdraw demands

to the social outcome of water governance. For the sake of simplicity, values are static during the simulation.

The typologies of households are defined according to the classification of value sets in the Schwartz Theory of Values. There are two pair of opposite dimensions. On the one hand, the pair of *self-enhancement*, which focus on self-esteem and the pursuit of self-interests; and *self-transcendence*, that concern for the welfare and interests of others. On the other hand, the pair of *conservation*, which stress resistance to change, order, self-restriction, and subordination of oneself in favour of socially imposed expectations; and *openness to change*, that emphasises the independent behaviour and readiness for new experiences.

There are four typologies according to the value dimensions that are predominant in the household:

- **E-O:** *self-enhancement* and *openness to change*. Households E-O value *power* (i.e. social power, wealth, authority); *achievement* (i.e. ambition, influence, capability); and *self-direction* (i.e. freedom). Besides its own welfare, these households think that the service must ensure the autonomy of households (they consider it is well represented by wealth) and, then, its own (financial) sustainability.
- **E-C:** *self-enhancement* and *conservation*. Households E-C value *achievement* (i.e. ambition, influence, capability); *power* (i.e. social power, wealth, authority); and *security* (i.e. social order), *tradition*, and *conformity* (i.e. compliance). Besides its own welfare, these households do not want any shock or policy that can put the institutions and the public service at risk (for example, a social subsidy, that they think that may jeopardise the financial sustainability of the service).
- **T-O:** *self-transcendence* and *openness to change*. Households T-O value *benevolence* and *universalism* (i.e. equity, environment, social justice, peace); and *self-direction* (i.e. freedom). Focusing on the social welfare, these households think that the service must protect the access to households while ensuring the preservation of the environment.
- **T-C:** *self-transcendence* and *conservation*. Households T-C value *benevolence* and *universalism* (i.e. equity, environment, social justice, peace); and *security* (i.e. social order), *tradition*, and *conformity* (i.e. compliance). These households believe that the service must provide support to vulnerable households and must not waste resources on respect to others who also need them.

There are two public influencers: *PI1*, whose values are *economic responsibility*, then *citizen autonomy*, and finally *equal treatment*; and *PI2*, whose values are *conservation of the environment, social justice,* and *protection of households' access to the service.*

Public Influencers' Satisfaction. *PI1* focuses first on the financial sustainability of the water service, that is the extent to what the service costs are covered by the water fees. When the service is financially sustainable, it examines the number of households whose utilities costs in relation to their income are significant. If the service is not sustained by the water fees, it checks whether social aid—which is a subsidised tariff for those households categorised as vulnerable—is active; in case there are many vulnerable households, it may blame that policy for hindering the sustainability of the service. *PI2* audits first the average water use of households, and then also focuses on the number of households whose utilities costs are high. In any case, a policy that establishes social aid for vulnerable households mitigates its discontent.

Notice that this illustrates that it is necessary to translate values into specific terms in the domain in order to work with them in computational models: for instance, *economic responsibility* for *PI1* is reflected by the cost recovery rate.

Households' Satisfaction. Households' satisfaction is divided into two components depending on the context: *service satisfaction* (i.e. household context) and *political satisfaction* (i.e. neighbourhood context). On the one hand, households use local variables within the context of using the service at home to decide whether the water service meets their standards or not. So far, as the ABM is basic, they only perceive the impact on their budget, and evaluate the service accordingly. For more sophisticated ABMs, they could include other locally-perceivable variables as access to the service, interruption of supply, water quality, water pressure, company intrusion, etc. On the other hand, households evaluate the world-state according to the values they hold. The political satisfaction components and framing is delegated to the public influencers, as they are capable of perceiving the whole world-state. *Households E-O* and *T-C* look upon both public influencers and make an aggregation, while *households E-C* and *households T-O* take into account only one of them (*PI1* and *PI2*, respectively). Eventually, they make a mean of the two components to elicit their global satisfaction.

Political Demands. Both public influencers may try to convince policy-subjects to diminish their water use by releasing information about the water use at the society level and appealing to be within a *normal* range. Notice that it is done due to different motivations depending on the public influencer (i.e. *citizen autonomy* and *conservation of the environment,* respectively). Only *households E-C* and *T-C* can support and follow this advise (because they want to abide by social norms). When the service is not financially sustainable, *PI1* may advocate for suppressing the social aid if it is active, or support to change the management model in case it is not (e.g. privatisation or terminate the contract for the concession). In contrast, *PI2* may advocate for establishing social aid to protect vulnerable households, or even demand to terminate the contract when the protection of the environment is unacceptable. Households may support these demands depending on their value profile and their level of global satisfaction.

4.1 Simulation Example: Gentrification

The population starts constituted by 200 households: 25% *households E-O*, 50% *households E-C* and 25% *households T-C*. Each month, households with the lowest income are forced to move out and are replaced by wealthy *households T-O*, causing that the original population is practically replaced in 8 to 10 years. Additionally, a policy that establishes social aid for vulnerable households—those whose water bill exceeds a defined threshold—is enacted at the start of the simulation.

As former residents are replaced by new residents with environmentalist behaviour, the collective water use decreases over time. Consequently, the service becomes financially unsustainable, since it has been designed so that a minimum water amount is used by each person (Fig. 3). Apart from this, new residents are wealthy enough, and therefore they are not categorised as vulnerable households (Fig. 4). This results in a period in which *PI1* is completely displeased (Fig. 5): the service has become financially unsustainable, there are too many households that are not autonomous—in the sense they have to face too high water bills in comparison to their income—, and too many households receive social aid. This leads *PI1* to demand for the suppression of the social aid, proposal that is supported by 10 and 20% of the population during a period of 2 years (Fig. 6). Nonetheless, its support decreases over time because newcomers' values do not align with the proposal—in Fig. 5 the average household satisfaction reflects *PI1*'s assessment. Anyway, as the population is being replaced, and although the financial situation of the service is only partially acceptable, the new residents are solvent and do not need social aid, which satisfies partially *PI1*. This world-state is acceptable enough to dissuade *PI1* to demand for the suppression of the social aid. *PI2* is satisfied because environmental protection is ensured—households use an acceptable amount of water—, there is a policy of social aid for vulnerable households, and newcomers access to the service is ensured (actually, they are wealthy enough to not be in a precarious situation); this political assessment is communicated to the new population (because they share values), causing the average household satisfaction to increase again (Fig. 5).

5 Closing Remarks

1. In this paper, we characterised a feature that is relevant for policy-making, which is social support of public policies and derived policy shifts. We have proposed to enrich agent-based models for policy-making with new affordances inspired by *second-order emergent social phenomena* (e.g. perception, aggregation, support, etc.). Further work should enhance the meta-model by considering interactions between policy-influencers in political arenas and more dynamic networks of relationships between *policy-influencers* and *policy-targets*.

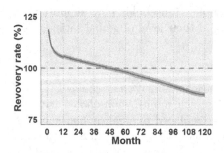

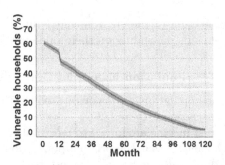

Fig. 3. Water service cost recovery rate (%) under a gentrification scenario.

Fig. 4. Households categorised as vulnerable (%) under a gentrification scenario.

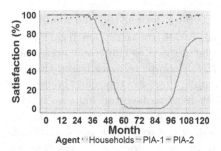

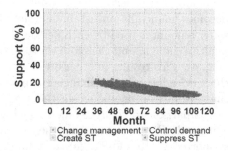

Fig. 5. Satisfaction of agents during the gentrification scenario

Fig. 6. Demands and support during the gentrification scenario

2. The simple model we propose may be used to formulate some common issues in policy design, for example:

Irrationality. Satisfaction models are *irrational* when they are *unfeasible*. For instance, an agent wants to satisfy two values at the same time that are directly opposed, being that situation impossible to be reached.

It is true, however, that *unfeasibility* is hard to be demonstrated. Indeed, some agents may invoke unfeasibility as a political argument to rhetorically attack other agents (in which case, it would not be *politically unfeasible*, but rather *politically undesirable* from the argument-maker's point of view).

When a *policy-influencer* holds a satisfaction model that is irrational, this would lead to a perpetual state of dissatisfaction, no matter the policy enacted. If these models are transferred to *policy-targets*, they are likely to be perpetually displeased too. This would entail unstable social scenarios, as the *policy-influencer* (or another one) could take advantage of the situation to make incoherent political demands (because these do not address variables of the relevant world, either intentionally or unwittingly, and consequently are ineffective to address policy problems).

Policy Local/Global Spheres Misalignment. *Policy-targets* might be incapable of perceiving the attainment of policy targets at the macro-scale, either because they do not receive the information by trusted *policy-influencers*, or because they do not have the values to consider these policy outcomes relevant. Nonetheless, *policy-targets* are aware of the local effects of the policy. If the local effects are viewed as negative (e.g. restrictions or taxes), but *policy-targets* are unable to perceive and value the effects at the macro level (e.g. air pollution reduction), this can lead to unstable social situations.

Limited Competence of *Policy-Makers*. *Policy-influencers* may evaluate the world-state using variables that the *policy-makers* in charge may not consider relevant because of their values. Therefore, despite sharing the same world-state, they perceive it differently. Consequently, *policy-makers* will receive the political demands as a reaction of the policy being enacted—thus, the demands have been raised due to political dissatisfaction of *policy-targets* and *policy-influencers*. In this case, the administration of the social space may become socially unstable.

3. Applications of this meta-model need to be complemented with fieldwork to build empirical value aggregation models. Such models should consider empirically elicited values, understandings, indicators and associated political demands.
4. Our proposal applies to hybrid systems where agents may be either human or artificial entities. In the hyper-connected society [5], human agents interact with artificial entities (e.g. virtual assistants, recommendation systems, etc.), and both of them may communicate with different *policy-influencers* (human or artificial). For instance, in the context of a household, a human agent is provided with a service through an appliance (e.g. laundry and washing machine). This device could register data of the user or the environment, and transfer it to a higher artificial entity, who could process aggregated data and then send additional instructions to those basic devices, acting as a *policy-influencer* (e.g. an order to delay a wash program to avoid peak flows). In some way, there is an exchange of information (and resources) between agents of different levels and hierarchies.

Acknowledgement. The first and third authors are supported with the industrial doctoral grants 2016DI043 and 2016DI042, respectively, which are provided by the Catalan Secretariat for Universities and Research (AGAUR). This research has been supported by the CIMBVAL project (Spanish government, project # TIN2017-89758-R).

References

1. Achen, C., Bartels, L.: Democracy for Realists: Why Elections do Not Produce Responsive Government. Princeton Studies in Political Behavior. Princeton University Press, Princeton (2016)
2. Aldewereld, H., Boissier, O., Dignum, V., Noriega, P., Padget, J. (eds.): Social Coordination Frameworks for Social Technical Systems. LGTS, vol. 30. Springer, Cham (2016). https://doi.org/10.1007/978-3-319-33570-4

3. Botterill, L.C., Fenna, A.: Interrogating Public Policy Theory. Edward Elgar Publishing, Cheltenham (2019)
4. Castelfranchi, C.: Simulating with cognitive agents: the importance of *Cognitive Emergence*. In: Sichman, J.S., Conte, R., Gilbert, N. (eds.) MABS 1998. LNCS (LNAI), vol. 1534, pp. 26–44. Springer, Heidelberg (1998). https://doi.org/10.1007/10692956_3
5. Floridi, L. (ed.): The Onlife Manifesto. Springer, Cham (2015). https://doi.org/10.1007/978-3-319-04093-6
6. Gilbert, N., Ahrweiler, P., Barbrook-Johnson, P., Narasimhan, K.P., Wilkinson, H.: Computational modelling of public policy: reflections on practice. J. Artif. Soc. Soc. Simul. **21**(1), 14 (2018)
7. Lakoff, G.: Why it matters how we frame the environment. Environ. Commun. **4**(1), 70–81 (2010)
8. Mercuur, R., Dignum, V., Jonker, C.: The use of values for modeling social agents. In: Quan Bai, Fenghui Ren, M.Z.T.I. (ed.) Proceedings of the 3nd International Workshop on Smart Simulation and Modelling for Complex Systems (2017)
9. Miceli, M., Castelfranchi, C.: A cognitive approach to values. J. Theory Soc. Behav. **19**(2), 169–193 (1989)
10. Noriega, P., Padget, J., Verhagen, H., d'Inverno, M.: Towards a framework for socio-cognitive technical systems. In: Ghose, A., Oren, N., Telang, P., Thangarajah, J. (eds.) COIN 2014. LNCS (LNAI), vol. 9372, pp. 164–181. Springer, Cham (2015). https://doi.org/10.1007/978-3-319-25420-3_11
11. Oishi, S., Diener, E., Lucas, R.E.: The optimum level of well-being: can people be too happy? In: Diener, E. (ed.) The Science of Well-Being, pp. 175–200. Springer, Dordrecht (2009). https://doi.org/10.1007/978-90-481-2350-6_8
12. Noriega, P., Sabater-Mir, J., Verhagen, H., Padget, J., d'Inverno, M.: Identifying affordances for modelling second-order emergent phenomena with the $\mathcal{WIT}$ framework. In: Sukthankar, G., Rodriguez-Aguilar, J.A. (eds.) AAMAS 2017. LNCS (LNAI), vol. 10643, pp. 208–227. Springer, Cham (2017). https://doi.org/10.1007/978-3-319-71679-4_14
13. Parks, L., Guay, R.P.: Personality, values, and motivation. Personality Individ. Differ. **47**(7), 675–684 (2009)
14. Perello-Moragues, A., Noriega, P.: Using agent-based simulation to understand the role of values in policy-making. In: Proceedings of the Social Simulation Conference 2018 (SSC 2018) (2018, in press)
15. Conte, R., Andrighetto, G., Campennì, M., Paolucci, M.: Emergent and immergent effects in complex social systems. In: Proceedings of AAAI Symposium, Social and Organizational Aspects of Intelligence, pp. 8–11 (2007)
16. Schwartz, S.H.: Universals in the content and structure of values: theoretical advances and empirical tests in 20 countries. In: Zanna, M.P. (ed.) Advances in Experimental Social Psychology, vol. 25, pp. 1–65. Academic Press (1992)
17. Stewart, J.: Public Policy Values, 1st edn. Palgrave Macmillan, London (2009)
18. Witesman, E., Walters, L.: public service values: a new approach to the study of motivation in the public sphere. Public Adm. **92**(2), 375–405 (2014)

A Collective Action Simulation Platform

Stephen Cranefield[(✉)], Hannah Clark-Younger, and Geoff Hay

Department of Information Science, University of Otago,
PO Box 56, Dunedin, New Zealand
stephen.cranefield@otago.ac.nz

Abstract. In this paper, we discuss some types of expectation that contribute to the behaviour of social agents, and investigate the role that these social expectations can play in the resolution of collective action problems. We describe our Collective Action Simulation Platform (CASP), a framework that allows us to integrate the Java-based Repast Simphony platform with a Prolog-based event calculus interpreter. This allows us to run simulations of agents who make reference to social expectations when reasoning about which actions to perform. We demonstrate the use of CASP in modelling a simple scenario involving agents in a collective action problem, showing that agents who are informed by social expectations can be led to cooperative behaviour that would otherwise be considered "non-rational".

1 Introduction

Collective action problems involve members of a community who must coordinate or collaborate in order to achieve a collective, rather than individual, benefit [10,13,16,23,33]. In the common case when the benefit is non-excludable (all can share in it, regardless of their contribution), this leads to the *free rider problem*: individuals can benefit from the collective action of others, while failing to make their own contribution [14]. Problems of this sort include coordinating access to a common resource pool (e.g. river water or a fishery) and collectively reducing carbon emissions from energy use.

Mathematical analysis of this problem has led to the conclusion that, in the absence of coercion or individual inducements, each community member's rational decision is to be a free rider [12,23]. This is a *social dilemma* whereby individual rational reasoning leads to a sub-optimal outcome for the community. In the context of collective access to a shared resource, Hardin [11] argued that the individual payoff from increasing personal use of the resource will outweigh any reduced value of the resource due to overuse. As this reasoning is repeated

---

Stephen Cranefield acknowledges funding from the Marsden Fund Council from Government funding, administered by the Royal Society of New Zealand.

The second and third authors contributed to this paper while working at the University of Otago. Hannah Clark-Younger is now at Soul Machines, hannah.clark-younger@soulmachines.com.

© Springer Nature Switzerland AG 2020
M. Paolucci et al. (Eds.): MABS 2019, LNAI 12025, pp. 69–80, 2020.
https://doi.org/10.1007/978-3-030-60843-9_6

by all resource users, the seemingly inevitable outcome is the ruination of the resource, referred to by Hardin as "the tragedy of the commons".

However, inspired by the observation that cooperative behaviour is observed in human and animal societies, researchers have proposed a wide range of mechanisms that allow the social dilemma to be broken. Holzinger [16] discusses mechanisms proposed across a range of disciplines (e.g. philosophy, sociology, economics and politics) and categorises them into (a) individual solutions based on internal motivations (e.g. altruism), (b) individual solutions based on rational expectations (e.g. the existence of social conventions), (c) collective solutions based on social choice mechanisms (e.g. voting), and (d) collective mechanisms based on enforcement mechanisms (e.g. rules and sanctions). Reuben [33] also discusses a range of proposed solutions, including the existence of private incentives for cooperation, changing the game to include (e.g.) repeated interactions, consideration of heterogeneous social preferences amongst the agents, the use of evolutionary and learning models to explain the emergence of cooperation, and the existence of non-uniform social network structures. After extensive fieldwork, Ostrom [24] identified eight principles that she found to be common to the governance rules of successfully managed real-world community resources.

Most prior work outlined above has made advances in the high level understanding of collective action by focusing on the very abstract mathematical models of *game theory* [18]. These models typically assume that participants select their actions simultaneously, and choose to maximise their immediate reward, with the reward structure defined by a payoff matrix. These models cannot be seen as sufficiently realistic models for human behaviour. In particular, there is a lack of consideration of the (bounded) reasoning processes that can lead community members to participate in collective action [33]. This research gap is significant given an increasing interest in the field of *social computing* [9,34], which aims to develop software that assists members of a community to collaborate effectively.

Our aim is to investigate the collective action problem by drawing on prior work on computational models of social reasoning, using mechanisms such as social expectations [8] and norms [10,15,38]. There has been little prior work in this area other than the work of Pitt and colleagues, who have developed computational models of Ostrom's principles for self-governance of common-pool resources [24,32] and on social capital [28–31]. The latter work investigated three forms of social capital identified by Ostrom and Ahn [25]: measures of trustworthiness, social network connections, and the observed conformance to the rules of one or more potential 'institutions' governing the interactions in the community. The results showed that choosing whether to cooperate based on a linear function of these social capital measures enhances collective action in settings where pure game-theoretic reasoning allows no polynomial-time algorithm for generating stable and socially optimal behaviour [27]. The three types of social capital studied in this work can be seen as means to coordinate the expectations of community members regarding the behaviour of others.

This paper elaborates on this intuition by proposing a novel model for collection action problems in which agents consider *social expectations* when deliberating about their action choices, and describes an agent-based simulation framework based on the model. An implemented group fishing simulation scenario is presented, and it is shown how cooperation can emerge when socially aware agents have knowledge of, and trust in, particular types of social expectation.

2   Expectations

Expectations drive our daily behaviour in many different ways. We hang our washing on the line in the morning because we expect that it will be dry by the afternoon, we turn up to work because we expect our employer to pay us, and we turn off our cellphones at the movies because we are expected to do so.

We can think of expectations as falling into two interesting categories—expectations about the consequences of our actions, and social expectations. Hanging out our washing falls into the first category, because our expectation is that the moisture will evaporate in the warm, dry air. Expecting our employer to pay us and turning off our cellphones at the movies are examples of social expectations, because they involve other people. In the first case, we have an expectation *of someone else*, and in the second case, other people have an expectation *of us*. We also expect our actions .to have social consequences: I expect that if I use my cellphone during the movie, I will be glared at and possibly not invited on another social outing by my companions. Based on these observations, this paper groups observations into the following four types:

Type A. Expectations we have about the physical consequences of our actions
Type B. Expectations we have about other people
Type C. Expectations other people have about us
Type D. Expectations we have about the social consequences of our actions

These expectations encode the rationale for agents to make decisions based on their previous experience and social knowledge [8].

Expectations are related to predictions: like predictions, expectations concern a belief about the future. However, we follow Cristiano Castelfranchi in distinguishing expectations as those future-directed beliefs that are "evaluated against some concern, drive, motive, goal of the agent." [5, p. 264] That is, expectations are predictions where we *have a vested interest in the outcome*.

Expectations are also related to obligations. We could rephrase our examples above to say that we turn off our cellphone in the movie because we have a social obligation to do so. In fact, obligations of a certain kind can be identified with social expectations (types B and C), at least for our purposes. For a fuller discussion of these relationships, see [8].

3   Reasoning About Expectations

Our research aim is to investigate the role of expectations in fostering collective action. Our approach is to build agent-based simulations [6,21] in a number of different collective action scenarios and vary the type of expectation-based social reasoning used by agents to select their actions. In this paper we consider a team fishing scenario, which is described in Sect. 5. To facilitate our simulations we have developed a Java framework that extends and specialises Repast Simphony [22] to support expectation-based action selection. This is described in Sect. 4.

An important aspect of expectations is their dynamic behaviour. Domain-specific expectations are created (or activated) when specific conditions hold. Once expectations are active, they persist until they are fulfilled or violated. As they represent constraints on the future, and the future is gradually revealed as time goes by, these constraints may (in general) be partially evaluated and simplified over time (this is known as progression). If an expectation is reduced to *true*, it has been fulfilled. If it is reduced to *false*, it has been violated. Rather than specifying these processes as algorithms to be implemented in our Repast application code, we choose to use a declarative mechanism: the event calculus (EC) [17,35], which has been used by many researchers to model the dynamics of social and institutional constructs such as commitments [7,37] and norms [1,2].

The event calculus is a logic-based formalism for defining the effects of actions and reasoning about how actions change the state of the world. This can be extended to track the creation, fulfilment and violation of expectations expressed using linear temporal logic [8]. A significant advantage of the event calculus is that it is directly executable: it supports *temporal projection*: an inference process in which a trace of events is combined with a logical description of the effects of actions to extend the trace with inferred action effects (social ones, in our case).

The EC supports reasoning about *events* and *fluents*. The latter are used to represent any type of state that can change over time. A fluent is associated with a value by a term of the form $F = V$; however, in this paper we only use Boolean-value fluents where V is *true* or *false*. The EC includes an *inertia* principle—the value of a fluent remains unchanged unless an action occurs that changes it.

In this work, we use EC rules to define the effects of social actions, with fluents representing the social state of the system. We extended an implementation of the event calculus (RTEC [3]) to include features of the expectation event calculus (EEC) [8]. This extension treats fluents of the form $exp\_rule(Condition, Expectation) = true$ specially: when *Condition* comes true, a new expectation fluent is created for the next tick. Expectation fluents express constraints on future actions and fluent values, and may contain the linear temporal logic operators $next^1$, *until*, *eventually* and *always*. The EEC's temporal projection progresses expectation fluents from the previous state to the current one. This involves re-expressing them from the (temporal) viewpoint of the *next* state,

---

[1] As we are using discrete time simulations, there is always a unique next state—in effect we are using a version of the discrete event calculus [20].

e.g. *next*(ϕ) is transformed into ϕ. When expectations become fulfilled or violated, this is recorded using special fulfilment and violation fluents.

4   The Collective Action Simulation Platform (CASP)

To support simulation experiments with agents that can use knowledge about expectations when choosing actions, we developed the Collective Action Simulation Platform (CASP) as a framework that extends the Java-based Repast Simphony simulation platform [22]. The key aspects of CASP can be summarised as follows. CASP integrates Repast Simphony with an event calculus interpreter to represent social state and to enable the use of EC rules to specify the social effects of actions. Agent reasoning is performed in two stages. A rule engine is used to determine actions relevant to the current state (including social state stored in the EC interpreter), based on rules associated with the agent's current roles. Then the agent selects one of the actions to perform. This selection may also consider the social state (e.g. an agent may get greater utility from performing actions that another agent expects it to do[2]).

CASP provides Agent and ControllerAgent abstract classes. These include a reference to a façade class that encapsulates an event calculus (EC) [35] interpreter (an extension of RTEC [3] running in SWI Prolog [36]). The Agent class also provides access to a Maxant rule engine[3], to support rule-based generation of possible agent actions. There are also abstract Institution and Institution-Role classes. To develop a simulation using CASP, the programmer provides scenario-specific subclasses of these four types of abstract class.

A simulation using CASP executes as follows:

- The Repast scheduler is used to run the controller agent's `step()` method once for each simulation cycle, followed by the `step()` method for each of the other agents.
- The controller agent runs one step of the event calculus interpreter to perform *temporal projection*: given the values of fluents and the actions that agents performed during the previous simulation 'tick', it applies a supplied domain theory (a set of EC rules) to update the Prolog fact base with fluent values for the current tick. These fluents represent the social effects of actions[4], as defined by the EC rules, as well the creation of new expectations from expectation rules, and the progression of existing expectations from the previous state.
- The controller uses the EC façade object to query the fluents that currently hold, and caches these. Other agents can query these via the façade.

---

[2] This would apply especially to obligations, which are specialised types of expectations. Currently CASP supports only generic expectations that a programmer can choose to interpret as (e.g.) obligations or commitments within the EC rules provided.

[3] https://github.com/maxant/rules.

[4] The programmer can also choose to model the effects of physical actions using the EC, or these can be modelled entirely within the Repast agents' Java code.

	CC	CD	DD
C	$r-c$	$r-c$	$-c$
D	r	0	0

Fig. 1. The payoff matrix for a 3-person threshold game with a threshold of 2

- For each non-controller agent, the `step()` method invokes an instance of the Maxant rule engine, which is dynamically configured with all the rules associated with some role that the agent is currently playing. The rules have a condition expressed in the Java-based MVEL expression language[5]. The rule outcome is the recommendation of an action considered to be relevant when the condition holds. The condition may include queries on the social state (in the EC engine) as well as arbitrary MVEL expressions. In general, multiple rules from different roles may be triggered, and the agent's `step()` method must choose one action to perform from this set of relevant actions. This is done using application-specific code, which may consider estimated action utilities and/or queries on the social state. Finally, the selected action is performed by calling a Java method associated with the action name. The action implementation may involve asserting an event occurrence to the EC interpreter and/or the agent adding or removing roles.

The programmer is free to add other logic to the controller and other agents, e.g. to look up references to other agents using the Repast Simphony API and to make method calls on them to pass on or request information (CASP does not attempt to provide an inter-agent messaging system).

5   Scenario

In this section, we investigate how expectation-based social reasoning can result in the achievement of collective action in the context of a simple group fishing scenario inspired and abstracted from a study of the culture of the Trobriand Islands [19]. In this culture, all men in coastal villages are fishermen, and are expected to participate in a fleet of fishing boats when a leader decrees that it is a fishing day. We assume that the success of a fishing expectation is dependent on the number of participants, but a minimum number of fishermen is required for the expedition to be successful at all (e.g. if the boats need to encircle a school of fish).

This is similar to an n-person *threshold* game [4, 26], in which there is a fixed cost c of cooperating, and the payoff is 0 if a cooperation threshold is not reached; otherwise both cooperators and defectors receive a reward of r. Figure 1 shows the payoff matrix for a three-person threshold game with a threshold of 2. The rows shows the payoff for an individual's action (cooperate or defect) dependent on the actions of the other two players.

---

[5] https://github.com/mvel/mvel.

A fundamental question in game theoretic analyses is whether a game has one or more *Nash equilibria*. These are player action selection strategies that cannot be improved upon under the assumption that the other players will keep their strategies unchanged. Strategies can either be *pure*, which always choose the same specific action, or *mixed*, which choose amongst the available actions using a fixed set of probabilities of choosing these actions.

Evolutionary game theory (EGT) studies the setting of large populations of players, who continuously over time interact in cycles of game playing then replication. During game playing, players are randomly grouped to play a given game. Replication of players (and hence their strategies) is then done in proportion to the 'fitness' of their strategies (essentially the accrued payoffs). EGT analyses seek to find evolutionary stable strategies (ESSs), which essentially are those that cannot be successfully invaded by other strategies [4].

Bach et al. [4] analysed n-person threshold games using the methods of evolutionary game theory. For the case when all players receive the same award when the cooperation threshold is reached, they found that depending on the relative payoffs for different outcomes, there is either a single pure ESS (*always defect*) or an ESS that is a mixed strategy as well as an unstable mixed Nash equilibrium.

Assuming the second case holds, this suggests that we should expect fishermen to follow a mixed strategy when a fishing day is announced. However, this does not seem to depict real social behaviour where some individuals may always defect or follow a mixed strategy, but others appear to become committed to the collective action and always cooperate. We therefore investigate how this state of cooperation could be explained by social understanding of the expectations created by joining fishing teams.

Our setting differs from an n-person threshold game, in that we do not assume that defectors receive a reward from the group activity. Rather, in line with a two-person stag hunt game, we assume the fishermen have a choice between fishing alone (for a small reward) or cooperating by participating in the fleet.

We have modelled this scenario using CASP. In our simulation, there are villager agents who have 'energy', which is decremented each 'tick' of the simulation—but they can choose to perform actions that increase their energy. The villagers do some reasoning to decide which action to perform each day (represented as a tick). At this stage we have not performed extended simulation experiments to evaluate the dynamics of populations of agents with different types of reasoning rule. Here, we demonstrate the use of expectations when choosing possible actions, and selection of an action given different personality types that are distinguished by the value they place on the social expectation rules (this can be seen as their level of confidence or belief in the accuracy of these rules).

The actions available to villagers are the following:

Fish Alone: Go fishing alone (and gain one unit of energy).
Join Fishing Team: Join the fishing team (which introduces some obligations on the agent and on others toward the agent).

Fish With Team: Show up to fish cooperatively with the team. If nobody else shows up, gain nothing, but if at least one other person shows up, gain 10 units of energy.

As the simulation begins, the agents are initialised with a random (but low) starting amount of energy. They are also randomly allotted a personality type, which will affect how they make their decisions throughout the simulation. The personality types we used were 'loners', who are averse to joining teams; 'shirkers', who don't mind being a part of a team, but are happy to shirk any duties that come with this membership; and 'cooperators', who will take the existence of a social expectation on them as an overwhelming reason to act accordingly (though only if there are consequences of not doing so). We, thus, essentially have only self-interested rational agents, but show that we can achieve cooperation on collective actions based on social expectations. Note that the logic we have implemented to select actions are examples of possible personality types; the strength of our approach is that it provides the ability to model and experiment with various individual reasoning rules that take account of expectations.

On every tick of the simulation, the agents reason based on a series of internal rules to determine the actions that are relevant to the current situation, and then select and perform one of these actions. As explained in Sect. 4, both these decisions can be influenced by the social state as generated by the event calculus interpreter, given a set of domain-specific EC rules. Figure 2 shows three EC rules that, at the start of the simulation, initiate fluents representing conditional expectation rules. The first states that if agents join the fishing team, they will expect to never be hungry. This is a strong expectation given that defectors could cause a fishing excursion to fail, but represents the personal motivation for joining a team[6]. This is an example of a type A expectation (one addressing a physical consequence of an action). The second rule expresses the obligation taken on when joining a team: one is then expected to always fish with the team. In our agent reasoning this is considered both as a type B and a type C expectation: from any agent's viewpoint it constrains both its own behaviour and also the behaviour of other team members. The third rule expresses social knowledge about the effects of a team member defecting from a fishing expedition—if the social expectation created when joining the team is violated, then it is expected that the defector will be sanctioned. This is a type D expectation.

Initially, the agents have the following rules to suggest relevant actions:

Fish Alone Rule: If I am hungry, I (prima facie) should go fishing alone.
Join Fishing Team Rule: If (a) I am very hungry, and (b) I expect that if I join the team, I will never be hungry again, and (c) if I know that anyone who joins the team will be expected to go fishing with the team, then I (prima facie) should join the fishing team.

---

[6] Further extensions to the expectation event calculus reasoner could allow more complex temporal expressions to be used, e.g. a given event should occur once within every occurrence of a recurring time period.

```
initially(
    exp_rule(happ(join(Agent, fishingteam, fishingteam_fishermanrole)),
            always(not(isHungry(Agent))))
    =true).

initially(
    exp_rule(happ(join(Agent, fishingteam, fishingteam_fishermanrole)),
            always(happ(fishWithTeam(Agent))))
    =true).

initially(
    exp_rule(viol(_,_,_,always(happ(fishWithTeam(Agent))))),
            eventually(happ(sanction(Agent))))
    =true).
```

Fig. 2. Event calculus rules for the fishing domain

Once an agent has joined the fishing team (if they ever do—loners prefer to keep fishing alone), a further rule becomes available as a result of taking on the fisherman role:

Fish With Team Rule: If (a) I am expected to show up to fish with the team, and (b) there is at least one other agent who is also expected to show up to fish with the team, then I should (prima facie) show up to fish with the team.

The agent associates a valuation with each action. Loners value fishing alone higher than joining a team (as they have no interest in the latter). Cooperators value joining a team more than fishing alone. However, their valuation of fishing with a team is affected by the presence or absence of the third expectation rule in Fig. 2. If the rule exists, their valuation of fishing with the team is increased to become higher than that of fishing alone. This reflects their knowledge of the social consequences of defection (we assume this rule of expectation is well founded, i.e. that sanctioning is generally performed when applicable). If the rule does not exist, then the agents become shirkers. Shirkers are members of the fishing team, but place a higher value on fishing alone than on fishing with the team, despite the social expectations that are on them.

When a simulation is run with agents who are all loners or shirkers, we see them falling into the everyone-defects Nash equilibrium, where every agent barely maintains their subsistence-level diet, but there is no collective action and so they do not thrive. However, running a simulation which includes some cooperators (agents who take seriously the social state—particularly the social expectations on them and on others—and trust that they will be enforced through a social sanction on defectors) results in the collective action of fishing as a team, and thus thriving due to the higher reward for all cooperators.

Our aim, here, is not to propose that our model of cooperators will explain all instances of collective action, but to illustrate the flexibility of our approach in modelling "non-rational" behaviour that is informed by social state, including social expectations. Indeed, the cooperative agents take the social state into account when deciding which actions are relevant and when selecting an action to perform, and this leads them to cooperative behaviour that would otherwise be considered "non-rational."

6   Conclusion

This paper has proposed that the social coordination needed to achieve collective action can arise from agents explicitly reasoning about the social expectations that arise in the problem domain. It presented an approach for investigating this proposal via agent-based simulation (ABS), using a simulation framework that extends an ABS platform with the ability to query rules of social expectations expressed in a variant of the event calculus. The framework also provides a mechanism for choosing relevant actions using decision rules associated with an agent's roles in an institution.

A group fishing simulation scenario that is a variant of an n-person threshold game was presented, and it was shown how agents' social personalities could be modelled by action valuations that can take into account the presence of social expectation rules. For one modelled personality type, the expectation that violations of expectations by members of a group would lead to sanctions was considered as a reason to value cooperation over defection.

Future work includes performing experiments with different combinations of personality types and investigating social learning mechanisms that would allow this type of socially aware personality to spread.

References

1. Alrawagfeh, W.: Norm representation and reasoning: a formalization in event calculus. In: Boella, G., Elkind, E., Savarimuthu, B.T.R., Dignum, F., Purvis, M.K. (eds.) PRIMA 2013. LNCS (LNAI), vol. 8291, pp. 5–20. Springer, Heidelberg (2013). https://doi.org/10.1007/978-3-642-44927-7_2
2. Artikis, A., Sergot, M.: Executable specification of open multi-agent systems. Logic J. IGPL **18**(1), 31–65 (2010)
3. Artikis, A., Sergot, M.J., Paliouras, G.: An event calculus for event recognition. IEEE Trans. Knowl. Data Eng. **27**(4), 895–908 (2015)
4. Bach, L., Helvik, T., Christiansen, F.: The evolution of n-player cooperation–threshold games and ESS bifurcations. J. Theor. Biol. **238**(2), 426–434 (2006)
5. Castelfranchi, C.: Mind as an anticipatory device: for a theory of expectations. In: De Gregorio, M., Di Maio, V., Frucci, M., Musio, C. (eds.) BVAI 2005. LNCS, vol. 3704, pp. 258–276. Springer, Heidelberg (2005). https://doi.org/10.1007/11565123_26
6. Castiglione, F.: Introduction to agent based modeling and simulation. In: Encyclopedia of Complexity and Systems Science, pp. 197–200, Springer (2009)
7. Chesani, F., Mello, P., Montali, M., Torroni, P.: Commitment tracking via the reactive event calculus. In: Proceedings of the 21st International Joint Conference on Artificial Intelligence, pp. 91–96. Morgan Kaufmann (2009)

8. Cranefield, S.: Agents and expectations. In: Balke, T., Dignum, F., van Riemsdijk, M.B., Chopra, A.K. (eds.) COIN 2013. LNCS (LNAI), vol. 8386, pp. 234–255. Springer, Cham (2014). https://doi.org/10.1007/978-3-319-07314-9_13

9. Erickson, T.: Social computing. In: Soegaard, M., Dam, R.F. (eds.) The Encyclopedia of Human-Computer Interaction, Chapter 4, 2nd edn. (nd). https://www.interaction-design.org/literature/book/the-encyclopedia-of-human-computer-interaction-2nd-ed/social-computing

10. Fehr, E., Fischbacher, U.: Why social preferences matter: the impact of non-selfish motives on competition. Econ. J. **112**, C1–C33 (2002)

11. Hardin, G.: The tragedy of the commons. Science **162**(3859), 1243–1248 (1968)

12. Hardin, R.: Collective action as an agreeable n-person prisoner's dilemma. Behav. Sci. **15**, 472–481 (1971)

13. Hardin, R.: Collective Action. Johns Hopkins University Press, Baltimore (1982)

14. Hardin, R.: The free rider problem. In: Zalta, E.N. (ed.) The Stanford Encyclopedia of Philosophy, Metaphysics Research Lab, Stanford University, Spring 2013 edn. (2013). https://plato.stanford.edu/archives/spr2013/entries/free-rider/

15. Höllander, H.: A social exchange approach to voluntary cooperation. Am. Econ. Rev. **80**, 1157–1167 (1990)

16. Holzinger, K.: The problems of collective action: a new approach. MPI Collective Goods Preprint No. 2003/2, SSRN (2003). https://doi.org/10.2139/ssrn.399140

17. Kowalski, R., Sergot, M.: A logic-based calculus of events. New Gener. Comput. **4**, 67–95 (1986)

18. Leyton-Brown, K., Shoham, Y.: Essentials of Game Theory: A Concise, Multidisciplinary Introduction. Morgan and Claypool Publishers, San Rafael (2008)

19. Malinowski, B.: Crime and Custom in Savage Society. K. Paul, Trench, Trubner & Co., Ltd., London (1926)

20. Mueller, E.T.: Commonsense Reasoning. Morgan Kaufmann, San Francisco (2006)

21. Nikolai, C., Madey, G.: Tools of the trade: a survey of various agent based modeling platforms. J. Artif. Soc. Soc. Simul. **12**(2), article 2 (2009). ISSN 1460–7425. http://jasss.soc.surrey.ac.uk/12/2/2.html

22. North, M.J., et al.: Complex adaptive systems modeling with Repast Simphony. Complex Adapt. Syst. Model. **1**, 3 (2013)

23. Olson, M.: The Logic of Collective Action: Public Goods and the Theory of Groups. Harvard University Press, Cambridge (1965)

24. Ostrom, E.: Governing the Commons. Cambridge University Press, Cambridge (1990)

25. Ostrom, E., Ahn, T.K.: Foundations of Social Capital. Edward Elgar Publishing, Cheltenham (2003)

26. Pacheco, J.M., Santos, F.C., Souza, M.O., Skyrms, B.: Evolutionary dynamics of collective action in N-person stag hunt dilemmas. Proc. R. Soc. Lond. B Biol. Sci. **276**(1655), 315–321 (2009)

27. Papadimitriou, C., Roughgarden, T.: Computing equilibria in multi-player games. In: Proceedings of the Sixteenth Annual ACM-SIAM Symposium on Discrete Algorithms, pp. 82–91. Society for Industrial and Applied Mathematics (2005)

28. Petruzzi, P.E., Busquets, D., Pitt, J.: Social capital as a complexity reduction mechanism for decision making in large scale open systems. In: 2014 IEEE 8th International Conference on Self-Adaptive and Self-Organizing Systems, pp. 145–150. IEEE (2014)

29. Petruzzi, P.E., Busquets, D., Pitt, J.: A generic social capital framework for optimising self-organised collective action. In: 2015 IEEE 9th International Conference on Self-Adaptive and Self-Organizing Systems, pp. 21–30. IEEE (2015). ISSN 1949–3673. https://doi.org/10.1109/SASO.2015.10
30. Petruzzi, P.E., Pitt, J., Busquets, D.: Inter-institutional social capital for self-organising 'nested enterprises'. In: 2016 IEEE 10th International Conference on Self-Adaptive and Self-Organizing Systems, pp. 90–99. IEEE (2016)
31. Pitt, J., Nowak, A.: The reinvention of social capital for socio-technical systems. IEEE Technol. Soc. Mag. **33**(1), 27–33 (2014)
32. Pitt, J., Schaumeier, J., Artikis, A.: Axiomatization of socio-economic principles for self-organizing institutions: concepts, experiments and challenges. ACM Trans. Auton. Adapt. Syst. **7**(4), 39:1–39:39 (2012). https://doi.org/10.1145/2382570.2382575
33. Reuben, E.: The evolution of theories of collective action. M.Phil thesis, Tinbergen Institute (2003)
34. Schuler, D.: Social computing. Commun. ACM **37**(1), 28–29 (1994)
35. Shanahan, M.: The event calculus explained. In: Wooldridge, M.J., Veloso, M. (eds.) Artificial Intelligence Today. LNCS (LNAI), vol. 1600, pp. 409–430. Springer, Heidelberg (1999). https://doi.org/10.1007/3-540-48317-9_17
36. Wielemaker, J., Schrijvers, T., Triska, M., Lager, T.: SWI-Prolog. Theory Pract. Logic Program. **12**(1–2), 67–96 (2012). ISSN 1471–0684
37. Yolum, P., Singh, M.: Reasoning about commitments in the event calculus: an approach for specifying and executing protocols. Ann. Math. Artif. Intell. **42**, 227–253 (2004)
38. Young, H.P.: Social norms. In: Durlauf, S., Blume, L. (eds.) The New Palgrave Dictionary of Economics, 2nd edn., Palgrave Macmillan (2008)

An Opinion Diffusion Model with Vigilant Agents and Deliberation

George Butler[(✉)], Gabriella Pigozzi, and Juliette Rouchier

Université Paris-Dauphine, PSL Research University, CNRS, UMR 7245,
Paris 75016, France
george.butler@lamsade.dauphine.fr

Abstract. In this article, we propose an agent-based model of opinion diffusion with collective deliberation. The model describes a process of collective opinion change that iterates over a series of dyadic inter-individual influence steps and collective argumentative deliberation. In contrast with other opinion dynamics models, we equip agents with the ability to use arguments and avoid attitude change when no serious argumentative justifications for opinions are given to them during social interactions. We refer to this as *epistemic vigilance*, which we grade on the number of arguments the agent possesses and on how tolerant she is to "message-source" ("argument-opinion") discrepancy. In addition, we consider the dynamics within a participatory context in which a subgroup of agents periodically meets to discuss the validity of certain pieces of information. Ultimately, we aim at creating a comprehensive model that describes opinion dynamics as a process combining abstract argumentation theory and bounded-confidence social influence. To these ends, we study the evolution and convergence of opinions, the emergence of extremism, and the correctness of the outcomes of deliberation in the model. We find that the opinion dynamics with vigilant agents yields a sundry of interesting opinion distributions. Moderate epistemic vigilance may be associated with steady states with a low variance of opinions that converge slowly as well as with scenarios in which all agents end up at the extremes of the opinion domain. The trajectories are determined by how sensitive the agents are to informational cues. We show that the way deliberation is organized in the simulations (e.g. amount of discussion per topic, time steps between each discussion) is a determinant factor of opinion variability, as it may predict the emergence of extremism or consensus. Finally, the correctness of the outcomes of deliberation improves as more agents get involved in deliberation and more group discussions take place.

Keywords: Opinion diffusion · Abstract argumentation · Agent-based modeling · Deliberation

1 Introduction

In groups, opinions are formed over interactions, conflicts, and affinities among the individuals that compose them. Opinions, as they carry behavioral

© Springer Nature Switzerland AG 2020
M. Paolucci et al. (Eds.): MABS 2019, LNAI 12025, pp. 81–99, 2020.
https://doi.org/10.1007/978-3-030-60843-9_7

dispositions, are crucial in understanding the dynamics of important processes of group life such as political crises, preference shifts, the rise and fall of interest groups and the like. Numerous models that seek to describe the dynamics of opinions in a group exist. They repose on the assumption that people respond to the messages they receive simply by favoring the positions close to their own and rejecting the most distant ones. Among the theories that are used to justify some of these models (leadership, social comparison, and commitment theories), we highlight social judgment theory (SJT) [21]. Social judgment theory seeks to explain attitude change in individuals after these are confronted with a position or an informational cue. The main hypothesis of the theory is that if an individual is exposed to a position close to her own, say within her *latitude of acceptance*, then she is likely to shift towards the advocated position (assimilation). In contrast, if the position is too distant from her position, or within her *latitude of rejection*, then it is expected that she shifts away from the advocated position (contrast). The theory has been tested in small laboratory settings [14].

Whereas the social judgment theory and other families of theories explaining attitude change (leadership, social comparison, commitment theories, social impact, etc.) have been implemented in the past [5,16,19], most fail to integrate finer levels of reasoning within the agents. Even if they are able to predict data and give insight on social phenomena such as the shift to the extremes [6], consensus formation and multi-cluster opinion formation [14], they do not take into account the argumentative and vigilant nature of agents - after all, a change in attitude may incur a cost on the agent. Indeed, evidence suggests that individuals do not process information in the same way depending on how engaging the information is. According to [4], high issue involvement leads message recipients to apply a *systematic response* to information validation. In responding this way, individuals actively attempt to comprehend and evaluate a message's argument as well as to assess its validity in relation to the message's conclusion. To avoid being victims of misinformation, individuals must (and do) exercise some degree of *epistemic vigilance* [17], which reduces to a thorough evaluation of the communicator, the content, and the consistency of the messages they receive. In this paper, we propose an implementation of an opinion diffusion model which takes into account a rudimentary interpretation of epistemic vigilance, and more notably of the cognitive mechanism known as *coherence checking* [17]. When an agent interacts with another agent, the one who shares her position is expected to justify herself with an argument. The receiver of the message applies epistemic vigilance either by refuting the argument or signaling the discrepancy between the emitter's opinion and her justification. The model inscribes itself into a generic paradigm in opinion dynamics that seeks to mix argumentation and opinion change as in [3,15,22].

In the implementation of opinion diffusion models, opinion change results only from pair-wise interactions. However, in a group, other ways of communicating and exchanging information exist (media, associations, debates, deliberative polling, city panels), especially in democratic ones. As an example of group deliberation, it is well-documented that deliberative polling plays a crucial role in explaining the formation and net shifts of opinion on policy and vote intentions, even though the direction of the shifts are usually confounding [8, 11]. When a group engages in deliberative discussions, the size of the group, the way it is organized, the topics and arguments that are advanced, and the acceptability criteria for the arguments may preclude a transformation of preferences [11] and play a crucial role in consensus formation [3]. In particular, extremism can emerge from these transformations because either the argument pool in deliberation is skewed and the dominant subgroups exert their influence on the minority [23] or the discussion protocols are not sufficiently committing [18]. Along with an opinion dynamics model with epistemic vigilance, we complete the model with an implementation of a public space for deliberation in which an evolving sub-group of agents discusses the validity of a sequence of pieces of information (e.g. policies, laws, statements) in order to inform a decision-maker of the group's view. In our model and in contrast with earlier work on opinion dynamics with deliberation [3], the changes in opinion due to deliberation are only experienced by the agents that deliberate and voting is not required to validate the discussed decisions.

The opinion dynamics we present in this article consists of a series of deliberation and pair-wise influence steps that may induce opinion change. The novelty of our approach is that agents demand justifications before shifting opinions, and when in groups, they deliberate (using arguments) to conclude on the validity of some piece of information. In the making, we observe if some stylized facts in bounded-confidence opinion dynamics models (bipolarization, uniformity, etc.) are obtained and study the different steady states of the dynamics. We look at how different ways of organizing deliberation affects the variance of opinions, the proportion of extremists, and the correctness of the deliberated outcomes by considering those obtained from a situation in which all arguments are advanced during deliberation.

The remainder of this paper goes as follows: in Sect. 2, we present the model, provide the necessary basics to understand its implementation, and we introduce the metrics of interest. In Sect. 3, we report and discuss our results; Sects. 4 and 5 are dedicated to related works and the conclusion of the article.

2   A Model of Opinion Formation with Deliberation

Let N be a group composed of n agents. A central authority (CA) looks to the agents for advice on whether to adopt or abandon a policy. As a result, the CA prepares a proposal $\mathcal{P}$ and advances it in tandem with an argument I that justifies it. I, or *proposal argument*, is perceived through how well it supports a principle $\mathbb{P}$. A proposal in the model is a sentence that indicates a way of attaining a goal or solving a problem. A principle, a rule or belief governing one's behaviour, derives from the notion of values - values seen as fundamental social or personal goods that are desirable in themselves [2]. Environmental protection and equality are examples of values; to always maximize welfare, to protect the environment, and to always vote Republican are principles.

Agents are called to discuss a series of proposals on the basis of their opinions or positions in regards to the principle $\mathbb{P}$. When agents discuss one-to-one, they are

$$\mathcal{D}(\mathcal{P}, I) : \boxed{\bar{d}}\boxed{\bar{d}}\boxed{\bar{d}}\boxed{d}\boxed{\bar{d}}\boxed{d}\boxed{\bar{d}}\boxed{d}\boxed{\bar{d}}\boxed{d}\boxed{\bar{d}}\boxed{d}\boxed{\bar{d}}\boxed{d}\boxed{\bar{d}}\boxed{d}\boxed{\bar{d}}\boxed{d}\boxed{\bar{d}}\boxed{d}\boxed{\bar{d}}\boxed{d}\boxed{\bar{d}}\boxed{d}\boxed{\bar{d}}\boxed{d}\boxed{\bar{d}}\boxed{d}$$

Fig. 1. A deliberation process. $\bar{d}$ and d stand for pair-wise and deliberative interactions, respectively.

subject to pair-wise influence; when they interact collectively, they are impelled by the results obtained during deliberation. A *deliberation process* $\mathcal{D}(\mathcal{P}, I)$ over a proposal $\mathcal{P}$ is a sequence of deliberative and pair-wise discussions that lead to a recommendation on the acceptance of $\mathcal{P}$ (see Fig. 1) and to a shift of opinions.

2.1 Argumentation in Opinion Dynamics with Epistemic Vigilance and Deliberation

Deliberation, defined as an exchange of arguments, may be modeled by confronting, eventually contending, arguments. Following Dung's abstract argumentation theory [7], let $\mathcal{A}$ be a finite set of arguments and $\mathcal{R}$ a subset of $\mathcal{A} \times \mathcal{A}$ called *attack relation*. $(a, b) \in \mathcal{R}$ stands for "argument a *attacks* argument b", meaning that argument a is in conflict with argument b. One says that an argument c *defends* an argument a if there exists b such that $(c, b) \in \mathcal{R}$ and $(b, a) \in \mathcal{R}$. One names *argumentation framework* (*AF*) the couple $(\mathcal{A}, \mathcal{R})$ composed of a set of arguments and their attack relation, which induces a digraph in which the nodes are the arguments and the arcs are the attacks.

A *label* $\mathcal{L}ab(a) \in \{\text{IN}, \text{OUT}, \text{UND}\}$ of an argument $a \in \mathcal{A}$ denotes the acceptability status of a in a deliberation process. Intuitively, an argument is labeled **IN** if it is accepted, **OUT** if it is not and **UND**, if nor **IN** nor **OUT** labels are applicable. Moreover, one defines a *labeling* on an argumentation framework $AF = (\mathcal{A}, \mathcal{R})$ as a complete function $\mathcal{L} : \mathcal{A} \rightarrow \{\text{IN}, \text{OUT}, \text{UND}\}$, $a \mapsto \mathcal{L}ab(a)$ that assigns a label to each argument in AF. A labeling-based *semantics* is a set of criteria that yields acceptable labelings. For example, if an argument a attacks an argument b, then an acceptable labeling should not assign the label **IN** to both arguments. Basic semantics demand labelings to be *conflict-free*, meaning that no two arguments that attack each other are labeled **IN**, or *admissible*, implying that the labeling is conflict-free and that for any **IN** labeled argument a, there exists another **IN** labeled argument c such that c defends (or reinstates) a.

The family of admissibility-based labelings goes from *complete* labellings, which are admissible labelings for which all labels (including the undecided) are justified [1], to *preferred* and *grounded* labellings which are complete labellings obtained from, respectively, maximizing and minimizing the number of arguments that are labeled **IN**. They capture properties such as credulity and skepticism in argumentation. For a more extensive account of semantics and labellings, see [1]. In our model, we represent deliberation as a dynamic argumentation framework embodying the group's ability to reach an argumentative consensus on the proposal argument at hand. With I = "To improve economic output, we need to diversify our production", a = "No, the economic situation will get worse", b = "We will grow in the short run, given the economic trends. We should

Fig. 2. Argumentation framework $AF = (\mathcal{A}, \mathcal{R})$ with $\mathcal{A} = \{a, b, c\}$ and $\mathcal{R} = \{(a, b), (b, c), (c, I)\}$. The labeling $\{\{c\}, \{I\}, \{a, b\}\}$ is conflict-free, a and b are undecided, c is accepted and I is rejected. $\{\{a, c\}, \{b, I\}, \emptyset\}$ is the only complete labeling obtained from the framework.

diversify while we can and ensure economic output later", and c = "Diversification will not improve economic output. We have to focus on maintaining the price of our stocks high", Fig. 2 provides a toy example of an argumentation framework that models one "step" of deliberation.

2.2 Deliberative Vigilant Agents and Opinion Dynamics with Deliberation

Every agent $i \in N$ has an opinion, a relative position or degree of adherence $o_i \in [-1, 1]$ to the principle $\mathbb{P}$. o_i close to 1 implies that agent i fully supports principle $\mathbb{P}$, close to -1 that she rejects principle $\mathbb{P}$. Agent i is also characterized by an *attitude structure*, a couple $(U_i, T_i) \in [0, 2] \times [0, 2]$ $(U_i \leq T_i)$ of positive reals known as her latitudes of acceptance and rejection, respectively, for informational cues. The intuition behind this structure is that there exists a level of relative discrepancy between agent i's opinion and the messages she receives from which attitudinal change is observed. For instance, if she receives a message that she perceives as being close enough to her opinion, then she will react to it either by scrutinizing it or by simply updating her opinion.

Let $\mathcal{A}$ be a finite set of arguments. Every agent i is endowed with set $\mathcal{A}_i \subset \mathcal{A}$ of k_i arguments. If $a \in \mathcal{A}_i$, then agent i knows which arguments are in conflict with a. Each argument $a \in \mathcal{A}$ has a real number $v_a \in [-1, 1]$ that stands for how much it respects or supports the principle $\mathbb{P}$. The value may refer to the conclusive statement of the argument as much as it may refer to the premises that conform it. $v_a = 1$ means that argument a is totally coherent with the principle $\mathbb{P}$, whereas $v_a = -1$ reads "argument a is totally incoherent with the principle $\mathbb{P}$". Finally, as to partly model the notion of epistemic vigilance, agent i is endowed with a real number $V_i \in [0, 2]$ standing for her tolerance to "message-source" discrepancy. The idea is that if she receives a persuasive message $m_j = (o_j, a_j)$ from agent j, she should perceive that the argument a_j is close to agent j's opinion (o_j) for agent j to influence her. We call the couple (V_i, k_i) agent i's *vigilance structure*. k_i is part of the structure because exerting vigilance also requires some knowledge of the argument pool and the attacks among the arguments. The smaller (bigger) V_i (k_i) is the more vigilant the agent is.

Agents strategically argue in favor of proposal arguments that are in line with their opinions. They are all (1) able to assess the degree of support for $\mathbb{P}$ of all arguments, (2) aware of the existence of conflict between any two arguments if such is announced, (3) sincere when communicating their positions to one another, and (4) unable to deliberate and participate in pair-wise discussions at the same time step. We assume that agents have an incentive to deliberate because they know that deliberation is an opportunity to undermine (support) a proposal they disagree (agree) with and obtain arguments to justify their positions.

An Opinion Dynamics for Dyadic Interactions Among Epistemic Vigilant Agents. Pair-wise interactions correspond to abstractions of one-to-one random discussions among agents. It is assumed that agent communication is argument-based or, in other words, dependent on the nature and validity of the informational cues they receive. When an agent communicates with another agent, she sends her opinion along with an argument that "justifies" it. If the recipient of the message feels concerned by it (the argument falls within her latitudes of acceptance or rejection), she applies a series of check-ups to either dismiss or react to the information (systematic approach).

Let i and j be two agents and suppose that agent j initiates an interaction with i. j chooses a *justification argument* $a_j \in \mathcal{A}_j$ that reflects her opinion in the opinion spectrum ($o_j \times v_{a_j} \geq 0$) and evokes the argument a_j as a justification ($|o_j - v_{a_j}| < V_j$) for her position o_j. i evaluates the argument's message and if it falls within her latitudes of acceptance or rejection, agent i applies vigilance to avoid attitude change. She may invalidate j's influence in two ways: (1) by stating the existence of an argument that attacks j's justification argument or (2) by stipulating that the argument she received does not concur with j's opinion. If i does not invalidate j's approach, then she is convinced of j's position, changes her opinion, and puts a_j into her set of arguments.

At each pair-wise influence time step t, two randomly chosen agents that do not collectively deliberate, say i and j again, interact with each other. Interactions are symmetrical so suppose that j influences i. If we denote j's justification argument a_j and $\theta_i(t, a_j) \equiv (\forall b \in \mathcal{A}_i(t), (b, a_j) \notin \mathcal{R})$ the formula stating that i does not know an argument that attacks a_j, i's opinion evolves as follows:

- **If** $|o_i(t) - v_{a_j}| < U_i$ **or** $|o_i(t) - v_{a_j}| > T_i$:

$$o_i(t+1) = \begin{cases} o_i(t) + r_{ij}\mu_i(o_j(t) - o_i(t)) & if \quad |o_j(t) - v_{a_j}| < V_i \ \wedge \ \theta_i(t, a_j) \\ o_i(t) & if \quad |o_j(t) - v_{a_j}| \geq V_i \ \vee \ \neg\theta_i(t, a_j) \end{cases} \quad (1)$$

- **Else:** $o_i(t+1) = o_i(t)$

where $r_{ij} = 1$ if $|o_i(t) - v_{a_j}| < U_i$ (assimilation of j's opinion) and $r_{ij} = -1$ if $|o_i(t) - v_{a_j}| > T_i$ (rejection of j's opinion). (U_i, T_i) accounts for i's couple of latitudes of acceptance and rejection, respectively, for informational cues, and $\mu_i \in [0, \frac{1}{2}]$ for the relative weight i gives to j's opinion, which is lower than the relative weight she gives to her own. Concerning argument dynamics, at every interaction in which i does not invalidate j's opinion, she updates her argument set:

$$\mathcal{A}_i(t+1) = (\mathcal{A}_i(t)\backslash\{c\}) \cup \{a_j\} \quad (2)$$

where c is chosen at random from $\mathcal{A}_i(t)$. The intuition behind this rule is that agents do not dispose of infinite memory and may "forget" or stop using some arguments as they receive new information. If argument sets were to grow too large, then the interactions among agents would become too computationally heavy.

If we abstain from modeling epistemic vigilance and the argument dynamics and replace v_{a_j} for $o_j(t)$ in Eq. 1, we get Jagger et al.'s opinion dynamics model [13]. We call it the *reference* model.

Spaces for Deliberation. Collective deliberation takes place on a table in which a CA fixes the deliberation procedure. The CA makes a proposal $\mathcal{P}$ and justifies it with proposal argument I. The CA controls the percentage of agents (n_D) that actively participate in the deliberative process, the labeling-based semantics (σ) used to assess the label of the proposal argument, and the number of deliberation steps to be held over the same proposal (m). Additionally, it also decides on the number (t_D) of pair-wise discussion steps in between each deliberation session.

Given a proposal $\mathcal{P}$, we denote $\mathcal{A}_I^d(t)$ $(t > 0)$ the set of arguments on the deliberation table at time t for the proposal argument I. The deliberation or debate protocol goes as follows:

- **Step 1**: The CA generates and makes public a proposal argument $I \notin \mathcal{A}$ $(\mathcal{A}_I^d(t) = \{I\})$;
- **Step 2**: The CA randomly draws a set $N_d(t) \subset N$ of $n_D \times n$ agents for the deliberation sessions;
- **Step 3**: Each agent $i \in N_d(t)$ advances an argument $a_i \in \mathcal{A}_i(t)$ from her sack that has not been previously advanced during deliberation $(a_i \notin \mathcal{A}_I^d(t-1))$;
- **Step 4**: The CA builds the debate's argumentation framework by taking all the arguments that were advanced in Step 3 and during the previous debates over I. It computes a labeling for the arguments using the semantics σ;
- **Step 5**: If the number of debates steps held for I is inferior to m, then the CA stops the debate and resumes it at the $(t + t_D + 1)$'th time step by repeating Steps 3, 4, and 5;
- **Step 6**: Otherwise, the discussion over the proposal argument I ends.

Notice that if the protocol is applied iteratively on $\mathcal{P}_1, \ldots, \mathcal{P}_r$ different proposals, each proposal $\mathcal{P}_l$ $(1 \leq l \leq r)$ is discussed m times by the same group of agents $(N_d(t))$. This protocol is reminiscent of empirically observed deliberation processes such as deliberative polling [8] in which the same group of agents meet multiple times to discuss a single array of topics.

Opinion Dynamics Due to Collective Deliberation. Opinion change due to deliberation results from the collective and argumentative deduction of the proposal argument's acceptability status. The latter corresponds to the labeling the group and the CA give to the proposal argument and may be associated with a notion of collective epistemic vigilance shared by the participants of the debate. Agents are focused on the result of deliberation; hence they update their opinions only if the message the proposal argument conveys falls within their latitudes of acceptance or rejection.

Let v_I be the proposal argument I's level of support for the principle $\mathbb{P}$. Given the acceptability status $\mathcal{L}ab(t, I)$ of I at the end of a deliberation step, $i \in N_d(t)$ updates her opinion subsequently:

$$o_i(t+1) = \begin{cases} o_i(t) + \gamma_i(v_I - o_i(t)) & if \ |o_i(t) - v_I| < U_i \ \wedge \ \mathcal{L}ab(t, I) = \mathbf{IN} \\ o_i(t) - \gamma_i(v_I - o_i(t)) & if \ |o_i(t) - v_I| > T_i \ \wedge \ \mathcal{L}ab(t, I) = \mathbf{OUT} \\ o_i(t) & otherwise \end{cases} \quad (3)$$

where $\gamma_i \in [0, \frac{1}{2}]$ is the relative weight agent i gives to the result obtained during deliberation, represented by v_I, when updating her opinion, which we assume lower than the relative weight she gives to her own opinion. Two important remarks follow from the equation: (1) potentially every agent that participates in deliberation may update her opinion; (2) shared epistemic vigilance prevents "unjustified" or irrational changes of opinion (e.g. if $\mathcal{L}ab(t, I) = \mathbf{IN}$, no agent updates her opinion due to a rejection of I).

The agents that participate in deliberation may keep some of the arguments they encounter during their deliberative experience. Since debates are abstractions of collective epistemic vigilance, agents only keep those arguments that have the potential to be "good" justifications for their positions in future interactions. Thus, at the end of each debate, every participant $i \in N_d(t)$ decides to keep an argument $x \in \mathcal{A}_I^d(t) \backslash \mathcal{A}_i(t)$ such that $\mathcal{L}ab(t, x) \neq \mathbf{OUT}$ (not rejected after deliberation), $|v_x - o_i(t)| < V_i$ (coherent with her opinion), and $v_x \times o_i(t) \geq 0$ (of the same sign as her opinion) from the deliberation arena. Provided that such x exists (randomly chosen if not unique), agent i updates her set of argument as follows:

$$\mathcal{A}_i(t+1) = (\mathcal{A}_i(t) \backslash \{c\}) \cup \{x\} \quad (4)$$

where c is a random element of $\mathcal{A}_i(t)$. We justify this rule like for the dynamics described in Eq. 2.

2.3   A Mixed Opinion Dynamics Model

In the mixed opinion dynamics models, we combine the opinion dynamics equations for dyadic interactions with those of the opinion dynamics in deliberation. At each time step, every agent $i \in N$ either participates in deliberation or in a one-to-one discussion with another agent and updates her opinion and set of arguments in the following manner:

$$(o_i(t+1), \mathcal{A}_i(t+1)) = \begin{cases} (Eq.\ 1, Eq.\ 2) & if \ t \not\equiv 0(mod(1 + t_D)) \vee \ i \notin N_d(t) \\ (Eq.\ 3, Eq.\ 4) & if \ t \equiv 0(mod(1 + t_D)) \wedge \ i \in N_d(t) \end{cases} \quad (5)$$

where t_D is the number of time steps between each deliberation step, Eq. 1 and Eq. 2 the equations that describe the opinion and argument dynamics for the dyadic interactions, and Eq. 3 and Eq. 4 the equations that posit the changes incurred by an agent from participating in a deliberation step.

2.4   Simulations and Protocol

Initialization. An argument pool $\mathcal{A}$ of 600 arguments is generated. Each argument $a \in \mathcal{A}$ is given a level of support for the principle $\mathbb{P}$ (v_a) drawn from a uniform distribution $\mathcal{U}(-1, 1)$. The attack relation $\mathcal{R}$ that gives birth to an ideal argumentation framework[1] (AF_ε) is established according to the v_as and is given a permanent labeling ($\mathcal{L}_\varepsilon^\sigma$) computed using σ = grounded semantics. We choose the grounded semantics because it yields a unique labeling. Argument couples with smaller absolute value ($|v_a + v_b|$) have a higher probability of attacking each other than couples with bigger absolute value. The CA generates a proposal argument I using an argument generation rule. Unless mentioned otherwise, the level I's support for $\mathbb{P}$ (v_I) is obtained from a uniform distribution $\mathcal{U}(-1, 1)$. We call this rule for obtaining v_I the *random rule R*.

The $n = 400$ agents that compose the group start off with opinions o_i drawn from a uniform distribution $\mathcal{U}(-1, 1)$. For simplicity, we assume $(U_i, T_i, V_i) = (U, T, V)$ for some $(U, T, V) \in [0, 1] \times [U, 2] \times [0, 1]$, $\mu_i = \mu = 0.1$ (as in [14]) and γ_i drawn from a uniform distribution over the segment $[0.05, 0.2]$ for all agents. Finally, every agent randomly draws a set $\mathcal{A}_i \subset \mathcal{A}$ of $k_i = k$ arguments such that $\mathcal{A}_i$ contains half of the arguments with $v_a < 0$, the other half with $v_a > 0$.

Observations. At the end of each simulation, we observe the opinion cluster formation and the following metrics to describe the dynamics:

1. **Variance of opinions**($Var(op)$): variance of opinions of the entire group;
2. **Proportion of extremists** (*Propex*): proportion of agents with $|o_i(t)| \geq 0.8$;
3. **Convergence** (*conv*): a simulation converges if before the 1000'th time step, the variance of opinions has been inferior to 0.0001 for over 100 consecutive time steps. It does not, otherwise.
4. **Time of Convergence** (T_s): denotes the number of time steps necessary for opinions to converge (in the sense of *conv*). $T_s = 1000$ if there is no convergence.
5. **Judgment inaccuracy or mean incorrectness of deliberated outcomes** (Q): mean score of the proposals that have been incorrectly labeled by the deliberation subgroups ($\mathcal{I}$ is the set of all discussed proposal arguments) in the simulation, $Q = \frac{1}{|\mathcal{I}|} \sum_{I \in \mathcal{I}} ec_I$, where ec_I is an *ad hoc* statistic measuring the group's ability to infer the correct labels of the proposal arguments,

$$ec_I = \begin{cases} 0 & if \quad \mathcal{L}ab_\varepsilon(I) = \mathcal{L}ab(t, I) \\ r_I & if \quad \mathcal{L}ab_\varepsilon(I) \neq \mathcal{L}ab(t, I) \end{cases}$$

where $r_I = \frac{1}{2}$ if $\mathcal{L}ab_\varepsilon(I) = $ **UND** or $\mathcal{L}ab(t, I) = $ **UND** and $r_I = 1$, otherwise. The correct label of any proposal argument I ($\mathcal{L}ab_\varepsilon(I)$) is obtained from the argumentation framework AF_ε that contains all arguments and their attacks. The smaller Q is, the better.

---

[1] The ideal argumentation framework refers to the framework in which all arguments and their attacks are taken into account in the evaluation of their acceptability status.

Table 1. Multimodal parameter domains for all simulations. The values that are fixed in the mixed interactions model, which we use for inter-model comparisons, are in bold.

Deliberation Procedure				
t_D	m	n_D	*Balanced?*	*Rule*
{1,**3**,5}	{1,**3**,5}	{0.02, **0.05**, 0.1, 0.2, 0.25}	{**Yes**, *No*}	{**R**, *S*}

Social Influence		Epistemic Vigilance	
T	U	V	k
{1.6, 1.8}	{0.2, 0.4}	{0.1, 0.25, 0.35, 0.45}	{4, 8, 16}

Simulations, Time Steps, and Stop Conditions. A time step in the model corresponds to an event step of dyadic pair-wise interactions and/or deliberation which results in agents updating their opinions. A simulation stops when the scenario converges or when the threshold of 1000 times steps is breached. We run the model 15 (procedural parameters sensitivity analysis), to 35 (mixed and argumentative model), to 100 (reference model) times per scenario on the parameter space associated with the initialization of the model and according to Table 1. An analysis of the chosen parameter space and the calibration of the model is left for a longer version of this article. Simulations and data treatment are performed in Netlogo 6.0.4 and R 3.2.3, respectively.

2.5 Expected Outcomes

We expect epistemic vigilance and deliberation to affect the correctness of deliberated results and play an important role in opinion convergence in the studied parameter space. As to improve the understandability of the dynamics and its outcomes, we express the following statements:

1. The model with epistemic vigilant agents should produce more extreme bipolarization and uniformity than its counterpart (reference model). The different levels of epistemic vigilance account for these phenomena:
   (a) Higher epistemic vigilance (lower V and higher k) should increase the time necessary for opinions to converge given any set of parameter values. The more vigilant agents are, the smaller are the chances that an interaction results in opinion change. More pluriformity steady states (compared to the reference model) should appear for this configuration;
   (b) Low epistemic vigilance (higher V and lower k) should result in either extreme bipolarization or uniformity (very high variance or very low variance of opinions). The intuition fueling this hypothesis is that low epistemic vigilance posits that very dissimilar agents influence one another even when their opinions are not as dissimilar (similar) as to fall within the latitudes of rejection (acceptance).
2. Deliberation should make convergence nearly impossible because opinion shocks due to deliberation are randomly distributed. As a result, any simulation that converges should take longer to converge when there is deliberation

Table 2. Models and their estimated distribution of steady states for all simulations. Ex. stands for the presence of at least one cluster of extreme opinionated agents. Mod. stands for scenarios in which there are none. Percentages are rounded to the nearest tenth and add up to 100%.

State Model	Uniform	Bipolar		3-pluriform		4-pluriform		n-pluriform
		mod.	ex	mod.	ex.	mod.	ex.	$(n \geq 5)$
Reference	0%	22.3%	0.7%	0%	27%	0%	20%	30%
Epi. vigil.	1%	29%	17%	0.4%	17%	0.1%	28%	7.5%
Mixed	2%	25%	11%	4%	18%	0.5%	29.5%	10%

than when there is none. In all cases, deliberation should reduce the amount and the stability of the observed opinion clusters;

3. Deliberation alone and any deliberation parameter that invites for bigger and more frequent deliberation translates into correct deliberated outcomes and reduces the variance of opinions and the proportion of extremists. The intuition behind this is that agents that reach deliberative consensus usually shift opinions in the same direction. The correctness of deliberated outcomes improves because more arguments are advanced during the deliberation process.

3 Results

In this section, we present a subset of the output produced by our model. We begin with a qualitative analysis of the opinion distributions in which we describe the steady states of the dynamics in terms of the number of clusters that emerge and of the proportion of clusters that harbor extreme agents. We end the section with a sensitivity analysis in which we discuss the effects the "deliberation procedure" parameters have on our observables.

3.1 Making Sense of the Opinion Dynamics with Epistemic Vigilant Agents

Thorough observations of the model's runs in the parameter space from Table 1 show that epistemic vigilance plays an important role in the dynamics of opinions. The first observations call for a fine distinction of the dynamics' steady states. For instance, we consider bipolarity (2 stable clusters), 3-pluriformity and, 4-pluriformity (3 and 4 stable clusters, respectively) as being moderate or extreme (having at least one of the opinion cluster in an extreme position within the opinion domain).

Table 2 summarizes our findings over all runs executed for each of the models. The first interesting result is that epistemic vigilance allows for uniformity and extreme bipolarity to occur, when they barely occur in the reference model. Moreover, the proportional number of cases in which there is bipolarization (especially for extreme bipolarization) is higher for epistemic vigilant agents than for non-epistemic vigilant ones. This is due to the scenarios in which the agents are ego-involved $((U, T) = (0.4, 1.6))$, are not too demanding in terms of

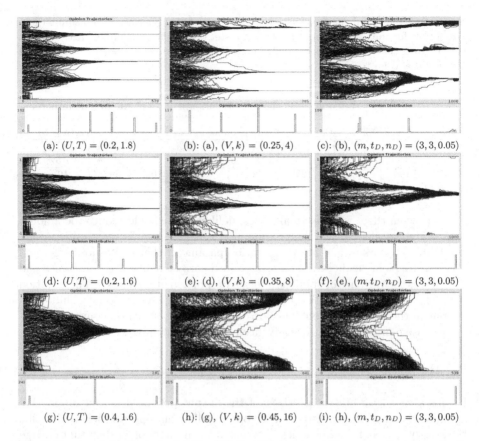

Fig. 3. Some opinion trajectories $(t, o_i(t))$ for 400 agents on the parameter space used for inter-model comparison (see Table 1). From left to right (columns), the trajectories for agents with no epistemic vigilance, with epistemic vigilance, and with epistemic vigilance and deliberation.

coherence checking $(0.5 \geq V \geq 0.35)$, and have sufficiently many arguments to communicate their positions $(k \geq 8)$. In these scenarios, small extreme opinion clusters form quickly. Agents easily accept the justification arguments they are given since they have a high tolerance to message-source discrepancy and may not have the necessary arguments to avoid being influenced – moderate agents begin to drift towards the extremes of the opinion domain. The result is a steady state with two clusters, one at each end of the opinion domain (see Fig. 3h). Deliberation only amplifies the drift towards the extremes because the agents are only affected by deliberated decisions that are sufficiently close to or far from their opinions. Moreover, they may retrieve stronger justification arguments during group discussion, which makes them more convincing and more prone to repel one another in pair-wise interactions (see Fig. 3i).

A second interesting observation is that epistemic vigilance allows for more 4-pluriformity scenarios than the reference model, and it dwindles in n-pluriformity

Table 3. Model-to-model differences for the mean values of the observations over all simulations (confidence level of 0.95). Entries in bold indicate a non-significant difference. T_s is computed only for the scenarios in which opinions converge. Values are rounded to the nearest hundredth.

Metric / Model	$Var(op)$	$Propex$	$conv$	T_s	Q
Ref. vs. Mixed	[-0.10, -0.06]	[-0.11, -0.05]	[0.64, 0.72]	**[-48.53, 6.36]**	[0.27, 0.28]
Mixed vs. Epi.vigil.	**[-0.04, 0.00]**	**[-0.05, 0.00]**	[-0.67, -0.60]	[110.06, 155.90]	[-0.27, -0.26]
Epi.vigil. vs. Ref.	[0.08, 0.11]	[0.083, 0.13]	[-0.08, -0.01]	[-133.61, -90.19]	**[-0.00, 0.00]**

steady states. This comes from the scenarios in which agents are less ego-involved $((U,T) = (0.2, T'), T' \geq 1.6))$, somewhat more demanding in terms of coherence checking ($V \in [0.25, 0.35]$) and have fewer arguments ($k \leq 8$). As observed in the transition from Figs. 3a to 3b, interactions that lead to contrast responses are blocked due to epistemic vigilance. Agents have trouble influencing one another. The clusters at the extreme of the opinion domain fail to form, and the handful of extreme-opinionated agents are absorbed into more moderate clusters. Similarly, the transition from Figs. 3d to 3e shows how epistemic vigilance impedes the emergence of a central cluster and yields a 4-pluriformity steady state. One possible explanation is that low epistemic vigilance allows for more social influence to occur than in the reference model. The agents that would end up in the central cluster in Fig. 3d are absorbed into one of the non-neutral moderate clusters, and some agents in the moderate clusters are pushed or attracted to the extreme clusters. As expected for these scenarios, adding deliberation into the dynamics reduces the number of opinion clusters observed throughout the simulations. Deliberative opinion shifts destabilize non-extreme opinion clusters and pave the way for the emergence of new, more moderate clusters as observed in Figs. 3c and 3f. Likewise, deliberation may be responsible for the emergence of extreme clusters, as presented in the transition from Fig. 3b to Fig. 3c.

Comparing the Models Using the Metrics of Interest. We examine the mean value of each metric over all simulations. We quickly infer that a high variance of opinions is an indicator of the presence of extremists ($\rho \approx 0.95$, $p < 0.001$). Thus, we study one or the other interchangeably.

From Table 3, we can say that epistemic vigilance allows for an increase in the variance of opinions compared to the scenario in which agents do not apply epistemic vigilance (reference model). This may be the case because a large number of simulations in the epistemic vigilance model result in an extreme bipolar convergence of opinions. Indeed, opinion bipolarization occurs when the latitude of non-commitment is smaller ($(U,T) = (0.4, 1.6)$) and epistemic vigilance is moderate ($k \geq 8$ and $V \geq 0.35$). Otherwise, a sundry of different opinion distributions appears (see Fig. 3) for which we can say little about the average variance of opinions over all the simulations. This diversity of steady states could explain why the proportion of convergent simulations for epistemic vigilance agents is smaller than that of the reference model. For the convergent scenarios, however, the model with epistemic vigilant agents is faster to converge. This was unaccounted for and may also be explained by the scenarios in which extreme bipolarization occurs (e.g. Fig. 3h).

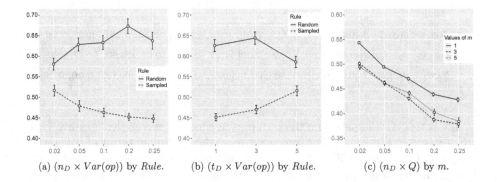

(a) $(n_D \times Var(op))$ by $Rule$.   (b) $(t_D \times Var(op))$ by $Rule$.   (c) $(n_D \times Q)$ by m.

Fig. 4. Curves of mean observations for the runs on the metrics (0.95 confidence intervals).

Surprisingly, adding deliberation to the model in which agents are vigilant does not seem to affect the average variance of opinions. Either the number of observations is too small to establish a difference among the two models (skewed confidence interval) or deliberation's variance increasing effects (e.g. emergence of extremism) cancel out with its variance decreasing effects (e.g. emergence of moderate clusters). Finally, the mean correctness of deliberated decisions is higher when agents deliberate, as compared to the implicit acceptance of all the proposal arguments in the non-deliberative models. The difference is of, on average, 27 incorrect decisions per 100 deliberated issues.

3.2   Sensitivity Analysis of Deliberation Parameters

For the analysis, we fix all the parameters that are not procedural to an intermediate value inspired from their domains: $(U, T, V, k) = (0.3, 1.7, 0.3, 8)$. The varying parameters are those entitled "Deliberation Protocol" in Table 1. In the analysis, v_I may be generated randomly (the R rule) or computed from a random one-third sample of the population (the S rule). With the S rule, the proposals discussed are, on average, more neutral. Also, the CA may choose to balance (have the same number of agents from both sides of the opinion spectrum) the deliberation table. We do not discuss convergence in the sensitivity analysis since the dynamics rarely converges when there is deliberation.

Number of Debates (m). The number of debates do not have a significant effect on the variance of opinions. We may attribute this to the fact that either the number of agents engaged in deliberation is too small to actually push the dynamics (which is surprising for $n_D = 0.25$) or because the long debates may usually end with undecided proposal arguments. What is quite interesting, however, is that the number of debates has a negative marginally decreasing effect on judgment inaccuracy (see Fig. 4c). The jump from 3 to 5 debates has a weak or insignificant positive effect on the quality of the deliberated outcomes. We expected that the effect would vanish when n_D was high, but it did even when n_D was low (strong substitution effect for the size of deliberation).

Proportion of the Population in Deliberation Steps (n_D). As expected, the more agents participate in the debate, the better it is for the accuracy of the decisions. The effect is marginally decreasing and seems to reach an asymptote at around $n_D = 0.25$ for each value of m. This means that if 25% of the agents are summoned to the deliberation table, then they are numerous enough to reach a stable and relatively low average level of correctness ($Q < 0.5$). We expected to find a higher statistic since the more agents there are, the easier it is to stumble upon an agent that would give up on a correct labeling to win the debate (see Fig. 4c). This could explain the marginally decreasing effect of n_D on Q. The variance of opinions over n_D varies depending on the rule used to generate v_I. A smaller deliberation arena implies a smaller variance of opinion only if the proposals the agents discuss are uniformly and randomly distributed. Randomness in the topic of discussion can lead to discussions on "extreme" topics and either pull (the proposals are accepted) or push (the proposals are rejected) agents to the extremes of the opinion distribution. Due to a small sample and effect size, however, it is difficult to assert the parameter's influence on opinions (see Fig. 4a).

Steps Between Deliberation Steps (t_D). The parameter has no significant effect on judgment accuracy. This is difficult to conceive since the more deliberation steps there are, the more arguments are exchanged among agents. We expected that the argument exchange protocol would improve the quality of deliberated decisions as it brings diversity to the deliberation arena. So, either some argument diversity is not needed to reach a decent level of correctness or the argument exchange protocol is biased and inefficient. To what concerns the variance of opinions, t_D's one-way effect is null. However, when considered in tandem with the rule used to generate v_I, we can see that if v_I is generated from a sample of opinions (S rule), adding more steps between deliberation sessions increases the variance of opinions (see Fig. 4b). Again, this is dazzling because we believed that the discussion over sampled proposal arguments would pull or push agents towards the center of the opinion domain, like in the transition from Fig. 4e to Fig. 4f, and reduce the variance of opinions.

Balance in the Deliberation Table. Strangely, balancing or not the deliberation arena has no clear significant effect on the observables. One could have thought a balanced deliberation process to be more consensual and more accurate. A possible explanation for this is that in most simulations one easily obtains bipolarization or 4-pluriformity. Consequently, asking for balanced deliberation (in terms of opinions) is almost equivalent to randomly drawing agents from the population.

Generation Rule for v_I. The rule used to generate v_I does not play a significant role in the correctness of deliberated decisions. The result seems natural since agents are focused on winning the debate and this is independent of the way the argument is generated. On the other hand, the rule has a clear and strong effect on the variance of opinions (see Figs. 4a and 4b). If the rule is sampled, the agents tend to reach more neutral consensuses and update their opinions accordingly. Indeed, the discussion of more neutral proposals calls for less repelling dynamics and more assimilation.

4   Related Work

Most models in the literature of opinion diffusion are interested in opinions because these have an influence on collective decision-making and on matters of social order. For instance, authors in [10] are interested in consensus formation and in how groups choose between two alternatives. Other authors shed light on the mechanisms that lead to the emergence of extremism [16], particularly when extremists are introduced in the population [6]. They show, using models of "bounded-confidence", that three different kinds of steady states (uniformity, pluriformity, bipolarization) are possible depending on whether the agents are sufficiently uncertain about their opinions and/or sufficiently connected to one another or when a significant number of them already hold an extreme opinion.

Another stream of discrete opinion dynamics models that explain the emergence of opinions is the family of models based on Latane's social impact theory [19]. In the theory, the agent changes opinion according to whether the informational impact she is subject to, which depends on the persuasiveness, supportiveness, and immediacy of the environment and the information she receives, is sufficiently strong. Simulations of the theory predict two emergent group phenomena: the shift of attitudes towards incompletely polarized equilibria and the formation of a coherent clustering of subgroups with deviant attitudes. Similarly, but in a continuous, more argumentative fashion, Mäs and Flache [15] present a model of opinion diffusion with arguments. Arguments are considered to be for or against a proposal and given an agent-dependant relevance in dyadic persuasive interactions. They also determine the agents' opinions and dissimilarities, as agents are assumed to infer their opinions from them. They show that opinion bipolarization can emerge from interactions among similar agents. In [22], a similar approach to argumentation and opinion formation is taken, but for the fact that they introduce different types of arguments, explicitly apply social judgment theory, and use survey data for model-to-real-world comparisons. Finally, in [3] the authors study the effect of deliberation, as an argumentative process for collective decision-making, on the opinion distribution of a population. They are interested in how deliberation timing, frequency, and size in collective decision-making processes affect the evolution of opinions, the correctness of deliberated outcomes, and the coherence between what is deliberated and a hypothetical majority vote. They show that an intermediate frequency of discussions and an intermediate size of deliberation lead to consensus and to a relatively high level of correctness. Our proposition in this paper differs from [3] in at least four key aspects: (1) an audience does not validate the final deliberated results through voting, (2) only the agents that deliberate are directly affected by deliberation, (3) agents are vigilant, and (4) they exchange arguments when they interact with one another.

When it comes to truth-seeking in opinion diffusion, the *funnel* and *lead-the-pack* theorems give sufficient conditions for truth-finding within a spectrum of opinions in continuous bounded-confidence models [12]. For discrete truth-seeking, authors in [20] show that learning about an exogenous correct state of the world (represented by bits) through pair-wise interactions is possible only if the agents are not too confident. In our case, correctly labeling arguments can be seen as a process of truth-seeking in which the correctness of deliberated outcomes should emerge from the system.

Back to opinion formation and abstract argumentation, Gabbriellini and Torroni [9] are the first to have originally and soundly merged opinion diffusion and abstract argumentation. They defined the agent's opinion as a function of the arguments she holds and the attack relation among them. They devised a focused peer-to-peer dialogue system of persuasion (NetArg), inspired from Mercier and Sperber's argumentative theory of reasoning [17], that used only abstract argumentation to study opinion polarization. Moreover, they used social networks and epistemic vigilance to define a dynamics for knowledge revision and trust, which we lack in our model. They showed that if a conservative belief operator in argumentation was applied by the agents when reasoning, then their dialogue protocol did not increase polarization. They also used the model to study the effect of network structure in the spreading of arguments, but were not particularly interested in notions such as the correctness of deliberated outcomes nor in tackling questions related to deliberation procedures and multi-level opinion dynamics like we are. That being said, their system is very expressive and helps position our work at the frontier between pure argumentative opinion diffusion models, opinion diffusion with arguments, and continuous bounded-confidence models of opinion diffusion. Apart from their work, we are unaware of existing literature on agent-based modeling that explicitly relates deliberative opinion dynamics and opinion diffusion through abstract argumentation as we have done it. This is why we see our model as a contribution to the social influence and opinion dynamics fields in ABM and as a pragmatic application of abstract argumentation theory.

5   Conclusion

The main objective of this article was to build and analyze an opinion dynamics model in which the notions of argumentative epistemic vigilance and deliberation, important factors in opinion formation, are successfully taken into account. The model revealed that asking for more deliberation and allowing for more agents to participate in deliberative instances guaranteed better deliberated outcomes. The effects were marginally decreasing on the size of the deliberating group and on the number of enacted deliberation sessions on the same piece of information. To reduce the variance of opinions and the proportion of extremists in a group, however, the pieces of information to deliberate on had to be chosen with care. If large group of agents discussed randomly chosen proposals, then the resulting opinion distribution became more polarized. However, if proposals were sampled to reflect part of the opinions of the group, polarization could be avoided. These results are partly consistent with findings in [14] and in [11,23], which stress that deliberation may polarize groups and may have a meager effect on shifts of opinion; and partly consistent with [8] where it is argued that deliberation moderates opinions. Undeniably, epistemic vigilance in opinion dynamics played an important role in the weakness of the effect of deliberation and in constraining the interactions among agents. In fact, the average effect of equipping agents with epistemic vigilance (because we could assume it low) was variance enriching and led to faster extreme opinion convergence. The more vigilant (argumentative) agents were, the less likely were pair-wise interactions successful in triggering opinion change and fewer opinion shifts occurred. As a result, opinion clusters took longer to form and moderate clusters could not merge at the center of the opinion domain. In contrast, when epistemic vigilance was low, opinion changing interactions occurred more often and among agents that were very dissimilar. This resulted in opinion bipolarization. Whether or not the opinions converged to the extremes of the opinion domain depended on the size of the agents' latitudes of acceptance and rejection: the bigger and smaller they were, respectively, the more likely the agents became extreme. The take-home message of this model is that if agents are open to discussion but decide to accept any argument as a justification of a position, then they may easily drift towards the extremes, even if and most likely because there is deliberation.

We can imagine many upgrades for the deliberative and pair-wise social influence implementations of our model. An important one would be to allow agents to update their opinions not only on the proposal argument's status but also on the status of the other arguments they observe during deliberation. Moreover, agents should not randomly forget arguments nor should they simply take in whichever one they are confronted with. It is important to draw inspiration from the existing literature on the mechanisms of argument diffusion within a group. Likewise, it would be more sound to have agents disagree on (1) the attack relation among arguments, (2) the strength or persuasiveness of the arguments observed, and (3) the criteria for assigning labelings to a discussion. Into what concerns the pair-wise interactions, trust, networks, multi-dimensionality of opinions, and learning are key elements to consider in the improvement of the model and to relax unrealistic assumptions. In conclusion, we need to explore different argumentation ontologies and opinion diffusion models (discrete, eulerian, purely argumentative) and find pertinent case studies to feed and test our models. This is essential to give credibility and visibility to our work and extend the use of abstract argumentation and deliberation protocols in opinion dynamics and social modelling.

References

1. Baroni, P., Caminada, M., Giacomin, M.: An introduction to argumentation semantics. Knowl. Eng. Rev. **26**(4), 365–410 (2011)
2. van Eemeren, F.H., Garssen, B., Krabbe, E.C.W., Henkemans, A.F.S., Verheij, B., Wagemans, J.H.M.: Argumentation and Artificial Intelligence. Handbook of Argumentation Theory, pp. 615–675. Springer, Dordrecht (2014). https://doi.org/10.1007/978-90-481-9473-5_11

3. Butler, G., Pigozzi, G., Rouchier, J.: Mixing dyadic and deliberative opinion dynamics in an agent-based model of group decision-making. Complexity **2019**, 1–39 (2019)
4. Chaiken, S.: Heuristic versus systematic information processing and the use of source versus message cues in persuasion. J. Pers. Soc. Psychol. **39**(5), 752 (1980)
5. Deffuant, G., et al.: Mixing beliefs among interacting agents. Adv. Complex Syst. **3**(01n04), 87–98 (2000)
6. Deffuant, G., et al.: How can extremism prevail? A study based on the relative agreement interaction model. J. Artif. Soc. Soc. Simul. **5**(4), 1 (2002)
7. Dung, P.M.: On the acceptability of arguments and its fundamental role in non-monotonic reasoning, logic programming and n-person games. Artif. Intell. **77**(2), 321–357 (1995)
8. Fishkin, J., Luskin, R.: Experimenting with a democratic ideal: deliberative polling and public opinion. Acta Polit. **40**(3), 284–298 (2005). https://doi.org/10.1057/palgrave.ap.5500121
9. Gabbriellini, S., Torroni, P.: A new framework for ABMs based on argumentative reasoning. In: Kamiński, B., Koloch, G. (eds.) Advances in Social Simulation. Advances in Intelligent Systems and Computing, vol. 229, pp. 25–36. Springer, Heidelberg (2014). https://doi.org/10.1007/978-3-642-39829-2_3
10. Galam, S., Moscovici, S.: Towards a theory of collective phenomena: consensus and attitude changes in groups. Eur. J. Soc. Psychol. **21**(1), 49–74 (1991)
11. Hansen, K.: Deliberative Democracy and Opinion Formation. University Press of Denmark, Odense (2004)
12. Hegselmann, R., et al.: Truth and cognitive division of labor: first steps towards a computer aided social epistemology. J. Artif. Soc. Soc. Simul. **9**(3), 10 (2006)
13. Jager, W., Amblard, F.: Multiple attitude dynamics in large populations. In: Agent Conference on Generative Social Processes, Models, and Mechanisms, pp. 595–613 (2005)
14. Jager, W., Amblard, F.: Uniformity, bipolarization and pluriformity captured as generic stylized behavior with an agent-based simulation model of attitude change. Comput. Math. Organ. Theory **10**(4), 295–303 (2005)
15. Mäs, M., Flache, A.: Differentiation without distancing. Explaining bi-polarization of opinions without negative influence. PloS One **8**(11), e74516 (2013)
16. Meadows, M., Cliff, D.: The relative disagreement model of opinion dynamics: where do extremists come from? In: Elmenreich, W., Dressler, F., Loreto, V. (eds.) IWSOS 2013. LNCS, vol. 8221, pp. 66–77. Springer, Heidelberg (2014). https://doi.org/10.1007/978-3-642-54140-7_6
17. Mercier, H., Sperber, D.: Why do humans reason? Arguments for an argumentative theory. Behav. Brain Sci. **34**(2), 57–74 (2011)
18. Moscovici, S., Doise, W.: Dissensions et consensus: une théorie générale des décisions collectives. Presses Universitaires de France-PUF (1992)
19. Nowak, A., Szamrej, J., Latané, B.: From private attitude to public opinion: a dynamic theory of social impact. Psychol. Rev. **97**(3), 362 (1990)
20. Rouchier, J., Tanimura, E.: When overconfident agents slow down collective learning. Simulation **88**(1), 33–49 (2012)
21. Sherif, M., Hovland, C.: Social Judgment: Assimilation and Contrast Effects in Communication and Attitude Change. Yale University Press, New Haven (1961)
22. Stefanelli, A., Seidl, R.: Moderate and polarized opinions. Using empirical data for an agent-based simulation. In: Social Simulation Conference (2014)
23. Sunstein, C.: The law of group polarization. J. Polit. Philos. **10**(2), 175–195 (2002)

Agent Based Simulation of the Dengue Virus Propagation

Letícia da Silva Rodrigues, Sóstenes Gutembergue Mamedio Oliveira[✉][iD],
Luiz Fernandez Lopez, and Jaime Simão Sichman[iD]

Universidade de São Paulo (USP), São Paulo, Brazil
{leticia2.rodrigues,sostenes.mamedio,lopez,jaime.sichman}@usp.cbr

Abstract. This work aims to implement a model to simulate the dengue
virus propagation, which is one of the main public health problems in
Brazil. In order to do it, we adopted a multi-agent based simulation
(MABS) approach. The agent model is inspired by the idea of compartments, widely used in classical models of epidemiology. The model was
implemented in the GAMA platform, as well as a classical model based
on ordinary differential equations. Although adopting some simplifying
assumptions, comparing the output of the two models made it possible
to validate our approach and to indicate that our model may serve in
the future as a basis for the development of more refined models.

Keywords: Dengue · Epidemiological models · Multi-agent based
simulation

1 Introduction

The main purpose of this work is to design and implement a multi-agent-based
model of the dengue virus' propagation, and to compare the model results with
some traditional deterministic epidemiological models. There are two benefits
from modeling an epidemic spread using simulation: to understand the mechanisms of propagation and to predict how the disease spread will behave in the
future, given a current state and possible sanitary actions. Moreover, we seek
to understand the effect of local conditions, like human typical trajectories, in
the disease spread. A multi-agent based simulation approach perfectly fits these
requirements, due to its dynamics, and this is the reason why it has already been
used by epidemiologists in many studies.

Next section gives a brief introduction to dengue, followed by the most common approaches to simulate epidemics in Sect. 3. Then, in Sect. 4 we detail our
model. Implementation details and experimental results of its application are
discussed in Sect. 5. Finally, we present in Sect. 6 our conclusions and further
work.

© Springer Nature Switzerland AG 2020
M. Paolucci et al. (Eds.): MABS 2019, LNAI 12025, pp. 100–111, 2020.
https://doi.org/10.1007/978-3-030-60843-9_8

2   Dengue

The World Health Organization (WHO) estimates that 40% of the global population is exposed to the dengue virus [10]. In Brazil, the first documented case was in 1923, in Rio de Janeiro [7]. Although in most parts of Brazil there has been a decrease in the number of reported cases, in the state of São Paulo there was a big increase from 2017 (4044 cases) to 2018 (8979 cases), according to data from Sinan (Sistema de Informação de Agravos de Notificação), a Brazilian institution that collects this kind of data.

The government and other organizations have been struggling in containing the spread of the virus, since its behavior depends on the its location, making it difficult to correctly apply the most effective policies against the mosquito and the virus infection. The main measures promoted are usually campaigns explaining how to avoid mosquito bites, how to prevent its reproduction and also how to take the vaccine shots. However, the mosquito and the population behaviors differ not only from one country to another, but also from rural to urban areas [6]. Therefore, it is indispensable the existence of tools that make possible to estimate the impact of a given sanitary action in a certain area. In this context, many epidemiological models are being developed to assist in the comprehension of the spread and resurgence of the virus and hence helping in decision making.

The dengue virus needs a biological vector to be transmitted. The main vector of dengue is the mosquito of the genus Aedes and the main species involved in the transmission in the West is the Aedes Aegypti. The disease is considered tropical because its proliferation is favored by the hot and humid climate, which are the ideal conditions for the vector reproduction. It is present in several regions of the world, such as Africa, Asia and the Americas [10]. The probability of occurrence of this disease around the globe is shown in Fig. 1.

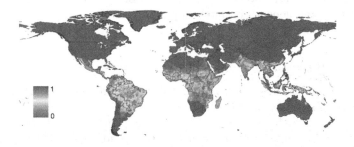

Fig. 1. Map showing the likelihood of getting dengue. The closer to 1 (orange), more exposed is someone who lives there. Source: [3]. (Color figure online)

The mosquito that transmits dengue and is well adapted mainly to the urban environment [7], it has a little less than 1cm in length and its bite does not cause pain or itching reactions. The female of this species is responsible for the transmission of the virus, since the male does not feed on blood.

The mosquito has a habit of biting in the early hours in the morning and in the late afternoon and usually does not get too far from its place of birth [9]. The mosquito is infected by biting an infected person as the virus can not be transmitted between mosquitoes or between humans. Symptoms include high fever, headaches, muscle aches, among others, and may progress to hemorrhagic fever and shock syndrome in more severe cases, where the patient may even die [6].

3   Epidemiological Models

Epidemiological models usually try to answer two questions: how a certain disease spreads and how it reappears in places not even considered in first place as susceptible ones. However, all models present a limitation regarding the reality, as they commonly try to represent a phenomenon either in a global (macro) or local (micro) scale.

For either of these scales, we can use the compartments theory. The idea of compartments is to represent the states of individuals. The most common types, which will be used in this project are susceptible (S), exposed or latent (E), infected (I) and recovered (R). Individuals in the state S are not carriers of the disease, but can be infected. In state E, they carry the virus but do not transmit it or show symptoms yet, which will only appear when they reach the state I, when they can also transmit the infection. In the R state, individuals are cured and immune to new infections. A number of different models, that consider different types of compartments, were proposed in the literature, such as SIR, SEI, SEIR, SEIRS, among others. The flow in the compartments happens in the order in which the letters are displayed in the model name. The model to choose will depend on the intrinsic characteristics of a disease. For instance, a SIR model states that individuals begin susceptible to the disease, then become infected and finally are recovered. The transition to the next state is usually not mandatory and depends on internal parameters of the model, which tries to resemble the reality.

3.1   Macro Simulation Models

This type of simulation focuses on a global level representation and makes use of mathematical equations, hence being a deterministic approach. This kind of approach ignores the individuals characteristics and the interaction among them. For instance, information such as age, sex, address and others cannot be used. According to [6], when using such a macro model there must be awareness concerning these limitations, since some of the individual characteristics may be of crucial relevance to the spread of some diseases. On the other hand, they are easier to implement and interpret. In [4], the authors concluded that it was not necessary to extinguish the vector in order to stop the dengue virus propagation.

The classical mathematical models are mostly based on compartments theory, and the change between one state to another is given by a system of ordinary differential equations (ODE).

3.2 Micro Simulation Models

In contrast with macro simulation models, in micro simulation models each individual is represented separately. The micro simulation approach adopted in this work is multi-agent-based simulation (MABS) [8]. A multi-agent system generally represents a complex system that has some characteristics such as nonlinearity and multiple levels of abstraction. Such systems contains agents that perceive the environment and act on them. These agents can be merely reactive to situations and also could take decisions based on their cognitive abilities. In MABS, there is no predefined algorithm that can predict the global behavior of the system. Hence, the interactions of agents at the individual lead to an emergent global structure. Therefore, the simulation needs to be performed several times, since it is non-deterministic. From the analysis of the distribution of these various results, it becomes possible to conclude something about the overall behavior of the system. Since the relationship between the inputs and outputs of MABS systems can not be explicitly defined, it is hard to verify and validate such models. In [2] and [6], the authors opted to consult a specialist in the field of epidemiology to validate the models.

Some previous works have reported multi-agent systems approaches in epidemics. In [6], the authors created a module able to trace a relationship between the spread of dengue virus and commercial routes in Asia. In [2], a model that encapsulated the characteristics of the north of Vietnam was used to describe the spread of the H1N5 virus. Hence, for the study of dengue in Brazil, it seems reasonable to use the same approach.

4 Our Approach

The main purpose of this work is design and implement a MABS to represent the spread of dengue virus, and to compare and validate its results with a mathematical macro simulation model. Both models will follow the compartments theory approach [1], in which we consider the SIR model for human beings, and the SEI model for the mosquitoes. Moreover, we are not considering any other life forms of the mosquito other than the adult, like eggs or worms. In addition, the birth and death rates during the simulation are considered to be zero, keeping the same size of mosquito and human populations from the beginning to the end. Figure 2 illustrates the compartment schematics for this study.

It can be observed that the passage of humans from susceptible to infected, and mosquitoes from susceptible to exposed, does not depend on those infected from their own species, but rather from the other one.

4.1 Mathematical Model

The equations set 1 describes the behavior of the model, represented in Fig. 2:

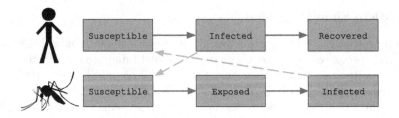

Fig. 2. SIR and SEI compartment flowchart for Human and Mosquito agents.

$$
\begin{cases}
\frac{dS_H}{dt} = -abS_H \frac{I_M}{N_H} \\
\frac{dI_H}{dt} = abS_H \frac{I_M}{N_H} - \gamma I_H \\
\frac{dR_H}{dt} = \gamma I_H \\
\frac{dS_M}{dt} = -acS_M \frac{I_H}{N_M} \\
\frac{dE_M}{dt} = acS_M \frac{I_H}{N_M} - \gamma E_M \\
\frac{dI_M}{dt} = \gamma E_M \\
N_H = S_H(t) + I_H(t) + R_H(t) \\
N_M = S_M(t) + E_M(t) + I_M(t)
\end{cases}
\tag{1}
$$

where S, I, E and R represent the number of individuals in a given time t, whether human (H) or mosquito (M), in the respective compartment symbolized by the letter. Table 1 describes the other model parameters, as well as their chosen values.

Table 1. Parameters of the model, their biological meanings and values.

Parameter	Meaning	Value
a	Daily rate of bites	0,168
b	Fractions of infectious bites	0,6
γ_H	Human recovery rate per day	0,143
γ_M	Mosquito latency rate per day	0,143
c	Mosquito susceptibility to dengue	0,526

These values were extracted from [1] and [4]. The human recovery rate corresponds to the mean time that a person recovers from the virus. The latency rate of mosquitoes is the average time to pass to the infected state.

4.2 MABS Model

In the MABS model, there are two types of agents: the mosquito and the human agent, each one with its own set of actions, described next.

i) Mosquito Agent. The mosquito agent is able to:

- *Move*: each mosquito moves in a random direction, and travels a random distance from its current location. Its position will always be close from the starting point.
- *Change to exposed state*: the change from the susceptible to the latent state can only occur if there are infected humans in the vicinity of the mosquito. The larger this number, the greater the chance to change its state. Being e the average bite rate per day and c the probability of a mosquito to be infected with the virus, we have $a * c$ the probability of the mosquito to bite an infected human and get infected as well. In addition, n represents the number of humans infected near the mosquito. Therefore, a mosquito changes from susceptible to exposed state with a probability p given by:

$$p = 1 - (1 - a * c)^n$$

- *Change to infected state*: the change from exposed to infected state depends only on the parameter γ_M, and the probability p for this to occur is:

$$p = \gamma_M$$

ii) Human Agent. The human agent is able to:

- *Move*: the displacement of humans aims to represent a common routine, from home to another destination, which may be school, work, among others. So every human has a residence and a destination and moves between these two points.
- *Change to infected state*: similar to the mosquito agent, changing the susceptible state to the infected state in humans can only occur if there are mosquitoes infected nearby. The higher that number, the greater the chance of this transition to occur. Being a the average bite rate per day and b the likelihood of a human being infected by getting bitten by a mosquito with the virus, we have $a * b$ the likelihood of a human getting bitten by an infected mosquito and becoming infected. In addition, n represents the number of mosquitoes infected nearby. The probability p of changing from susceptible to infected state is given by:

$$p = 1 - (1 - a * b)^n$$

- *Change to recovered state*: the change from infected to recovered state depends only on the parameter γ_H, and the probability p for this to occur is given by:

$$p = \gamma_H$$

4.3   Simulation Cycle

Each simulation cycle represents a duration of 12 h in real time. In the mathematical model, the number of humans in each of the states (susceptible, exposed or infected) is calculated at each cycle. In the agent-based model, at each cycle all agents perform their specific actions. In addition, the human agent can also have its destiny changed (from residence to school/work or vice-versa). The destination of humans is represented by a third type of agent, called immobile agent. Thus, at each cycle, an immobile agent checks if there is any human agent within its area. If it is the case, the immobile agent changes the objective destination of the human agent for the next cycle.

5   Implementation and Experiments

5.1   Technical Details

The implementation of the models was developed in the GAMA platform, which is specifically designed for MABS [5]. This platform makes it possible to visualize geographically the behavior of the agents on a map, as shown in Fig. 3.

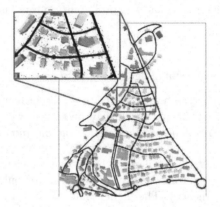

Fig. 3. A view in the GAMA platform using a simulated geographical localization. (Color figure online)

In the map, green means susceptible, yellow represents exposed, red indicates infected and blue means recovered. In order to analyze the output data from both models, we used R as the programming language in RStudio. After every simulation, we also validated the model with some specialists in the field of epidemiology.

5.2   Experiments

Three tests were performed, varying only the initial number of infected mosquito-type agents at the beginning of the simulation. Tables 2 and 3 show the initial amounts of each agent that were used in the simulations.

The comparative analysis was based considering the number of infected human agents.

Table 2. Model input variables for the Human agent.

Human (State)	Initial amount
Susceptible	495
Infected	5
Recovered	0

Table 3. Model input variables for the Mosquito agent.

Mosquito (State)	Initial amount		
	Test 1	Test 2	Test 3
Susceptible	9000	9900	9990
Exposed	0	0	0
Infected	1000	100	10

Scenario 1: High Rate of Infected of Mosquito Agents. In this first test, 10% of all mosquitoes were infected from the start. Figure 4 shows the simulation results for the mathematical model (ODE) and Fig. 5 for the multi-agent based simulation model (MABS).

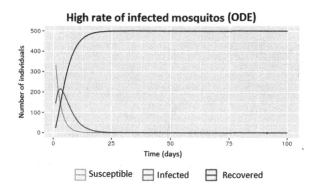

Fig. 4. Result of the ODE model with high rate of infected mosquitoes.

In Fig. 5, as in the next ones to be displayed for the other tests, the full line represents the mean of the simulations and the dashed lines, the standard deviation. In the case of the ODE simulation, shown in Fig. 4, the full lines show the result of the equations set 1. We can observe that in this experiment, all the curves are similar, indicating that all individuals were infected and later entered the recovered state. The peak that occurs is characteristic of an epidemic that occurred in both models. Thus, the global epidemic behavior of the two models may be considered equivalent.

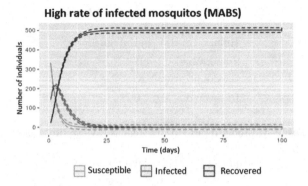

Fig. 5. Result of the MABS model with high rate of infected mosquitoes.

Scenario 2: Medium Rate of Infected of Mosquito Agents. In this second test, only 1% of all mosquitoes were infected from the start. Figure 6 shows the simulation results for the mathematical model (ODE) and Fig. 7 for the multi-agent based simulation model (MABS).

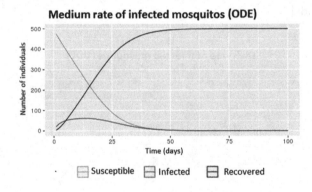

Fig. 6. Result of the ODE model with medium rate of infected mosquitoes.

The main difference between curves lies in the number of susceptible and recovered individuals. It is observed that all individuals pass from the first to the last state in the ODE model, but not in the MABS model. Observing the equations set 1, which represent the compartments, it is easy to see why this occurs in the ODE model. As shown in Fig. 2, which represents this model, for the human agents there is no exit transition from the recovered state. Hence, all individuals arriving in that state remain in it. Combining this with the fact that there are no entries of new individuals nor exits during a simulation, and that the transitions occur towards the recovered state, we have that at some point all human agents will reach that state.

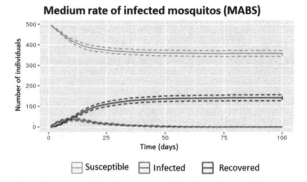

Fig. 7. Result of the MABS model with medium rate of infected mosquitoes.

The same behavior, however, does not occur in the MABS model. One possible justification is due to the agents' movement behavior and the possibility of including their location information at any time of the simulation. As they always move within the same region, vectors do not always spread the disease to uninfected areas nor do humans contaminate mosquitoes from other regions after a certain interval since the beginning of the experiment. This result is compatible with the one obtained by [6]. In this case, a positive correlation was observed between the increase in the number of dengue cases and the increase in commercial relations between some Asian countries. The hypothesis is that greater human displacements enable the virus to reach a larger region. Thus, by doing the opposite, which is, by limiting the area covered by the agents, we would be limiting also the spread of the virus. In addition, comparing the MABS results produced in this test with those produced in the first experiment, we can notice that the final amount of recovered humans is lower when the initial number of infected mosquitoes is also lower. This can be considered as an expected result, since fewer people were infected. In addition, one can see again an equivalence between the curves representing the infected individuals. There is a small increase in the number of cases at the beginning, which soon stabilizes.

Scenario 3: Low Rate of Infected of Mosquito Agents. In this last test, the number of mosquitoes that were infected from the start is even smaller, with a value of 0.1%. Figure 8 depicts the simulation results for the mathematical model (ODE) and Fig. 9 for multi-agent based simulation model (MABS).

As in the previous case, the fact that the movement of agents is limited to one region also limits the proliferation of the disease. This effect is even more evident in this test, since the number of susceptible and recovered humans has very little variation during the simulation. In addition, the curves of infected humans are also similar, with few cases of the disease, which is expected given the small number of infected mosquitoes.

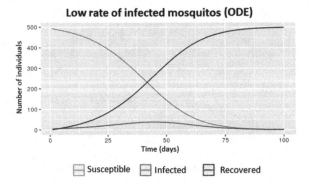

Fig. 8. Result of the ODE model with low rate of infected mosquitoes.

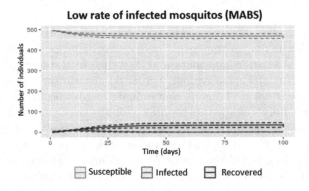

Fig. 9. Result of MABS model with low rate of infected mosquitoes.

6   Conclusions and Further Work

This work aimed to design a model of the spread of dengue virus using a multi-agent based simulation approach. The model was implemented, representing a basic and simplified version of how the virus propagates.

The comparison between the classical mathematical model and the multi-agent based model showed that the second technique can lead the system to the expected global behavior, since in the three studied cases, the profiles of the disease propagation (infected curves) were similar. Therefore, we obtained the same macro behavior when defining the interactions between the agents at the micro level.

This conclusion is significant because it indicates that multi-agent models can represent reality at least as well as the classical models. Moreover, as their capacity of representation is much more detailed, they can take into account the heterogeneity of the population and characteristics of the environment, among others. Hence, agent-based models have a greater chance of being more faithful than models solely based on mathematical equations.

Although being able to reach this conclusion, the current model is still very simplified. Taking into account its current state and drawing on the bibliography, the following items are proposed for a possible future evolution of the project: *(i)* inclusion of birth and death rates in humans and mosquitoes, *(ii)* inclusion of other mosquito life forms, such as eggs and larvae, *(iii)* use of real geographical data, *(iv)* use of geographical information (such as urban or rural areas) to adapt the mechanisms of propagation and *(v)* variation of the mosquito population due to the season.

Thus, we consider this work as an initial contribution to public policies, aiming to obtain in the future a model closer to the reality, and that can serve as a decision tool to mitigate the spread of this disease.

References

1. Amaku, M., Azevedo, F., Burattini, M., Coutinho, F., Lopez, L., Massad, E.: Interpretations and pitfalls in modelling vector-transmitted infections. Epidemiol. Infect. **143**(9), 1803–1815 (2015)
2. Amouroux, E., Desvaux, S., Drogoul, A.: Towards virtual epidemiology: an agent-based approach to the modeling of H5N1 propagation and persistence in North-Vietnam. In: Bui, T.D., Ho, T.V., Ha, Q.T. (eds.) PRIMA 2008. LNCS (LNAI), vol. 5357, pp. 26–33. Springer, Heidelberg (2008). https://doi.org/10.1007/978-3-540-89674-6_6
3. Bhatt, S., et al.: The global distribution and burden of dengue. Nature **496**(7446), 504 (2013)
4. Burattini, M., et al.: Modelling the control strategies against dengue in Singapore. Epidemiol. Infect. **136**(3), 309–319 (2008)
5. Grignard, A., Taillandier, P., Gaudou, B., Vo, D.A., Huynh, N.Q., Drogoul, A.: GAMA 1.6: advancing the art of complex agent-based modeling and simulation. In: Boella, G., Elkind, E., Savarimuthu, B.T.R., Dignum, F., Purvis, M.K. (eds.) PRIMA 2013. LNCS (LNAI), vol. 8291, pp. 117–131. Springer, Heidelberg (2013). https://doi.org/10.1007/978-3-642-44927-7_9
6. Philippon, D., et al.: Exploring trade and health policies influence on dengue spread with an agent-based model. In: Nardin, L.G., Antunes, L. (eds.) MABS 2016. LNCS (LNAI), vol. 10399, pp. 111–127. Springer, Cham (2017). https://doi.org/10.1007/978-3-319-67477-3_6
7. Pontes, R.J., Ruffino-Netto, A.: Dengue em localidade urbana da região sudeste do Brasil: aspectos epidemiológicos. Revista de Saúde Pública **28**, 218–227 (1994)
8. Sichman, J.S.: Operationalizing complex systems. In: Furtado, B.A., Sakowski, P.A.M, Tóvolli, M.H. (eds.) Modeling Complex Systems for Public Policies, pp. 85–123. IPEA, Brasilia (2015)
9. Silva, J.S., Scopel, I., et al.: A dengue no brasil e as políticas de combate ao aedes aegypti: da tentativa de erradicação às políticas de controle. Hygeia: Revista Brasileira de Geografia Meédica e da Saúde **4**(6) (2008)
10. Singhi, S., Kissoon, N., Bansal, A.: Dengue and dengue hemorrhagic fever: management issues in an intensive care unit. J. Pediatr. **83**(2), S22–S35 (2007)

Agents with Dynamic Social Norms

Samaneh Heidari[1]([✉]), Nanda Wijermans[2][iD], and Frank Dignum[1,3]

[1] Utrecht University, Utrecht, The Netherlands
{s.heidari,f.p.m.dignum}@uu.nl
[2] Stockholm University, Stockholm, Sweden
nanda.wijermans@su.se
[3] Umeå University, Umeå, Sweden
frank.dignum@umu.se

Abstract. Social norms are important as societal agreements of acceptable behavior. They can be seen as flexible, but stable constraints on individual behavior. However, social norms themselves are not completely static. Norms emerge from dynamic environments and changing agent populations. They adapt and in the end also get abrogated. Although norm emergence has received attention in the literature, its focus is mainly describing the rise of new norms based on individual preferences and punishments on violations. This explanation works for environments where personal preferences are stable and known. In this paper, we argue that values are the stable concepts that allow for explaining norm change in situations where agents can move between social groups in a dynamic environment (as is the case in most realistic social simulations for policy support). Values thus reflect the stable concept that those are shared between the agents of a group and can direct norm emergence, adaptation, and abrogation. We present the norm framework that enables describing and modeling value and situation based norm change and demonstrate its potential application using a simple example.

Keywords: Social norm · Social norm dynamics · Norm framework · Value based norms · Personal values

1 Introduction

Social phenomena are part of our thinking [11]. Therefore, it is mandatory to consider social aspects to study decision making and system behavior. Especially, if the purpose of the study is to explore the mutual effects of micro-level decisions and macro-level behavior of a system. Among different social aspects, we are interested in studying social norms, as norms play an important role in guiding all human societies [6]. Social norms are more important to study and consider in the absence of a central monitor/control [15].

Considerable research effort has been dedicated to developing models, architectures, and theories that concern social norms in making decisions. However, there are some points that have been omitted in the research efforts in two main

© Springer Nature Switzerland AG 2020
M. Paolucci et al. (Eds.): MABS 2019, LNAI 12025, pp. 112–124, 2020.
https://doi.org/10.1007/978-3-030-60843-9_9

issues: putting the focus on norm reactivity to environmental changes without regard for factors that drive norm stability, and favoring implicit, rather than explicit, representations of norms.

Studying the reactivity and stability of social norms cannot be effective without considering values, an element which is lacking in the previous works. In the absence of any stabilizing factors, modelled norms might quickly react to any change. However, many real norms remain rather stable over long periods of time due to their connection to fundamental values, which are, by their nature shared between groups of people and very stable over a person's lifespan. As for the issue of norm representation, researchers assume that social norms are explicitly defined in advance and use norms as constraints. Such an assumption is useful for simplifying the study of the effects of specific norms in a given scenario, but takes away the possibility of studying norm dynamics (such as norm emergence) and norm recognition [14]. Social norms are distributed concepts rather than central. Each person might have his own interpretation of a social norm.

The simulation of social norms and their effects on decision making and on the behavior of the system has gained much interest in the field of social simulation. Therefore, we believe that a framework that deals with values and norm dynamics is relevant for many social simulations. We introduce a normative framework that covers key dynamics of social norms, their effect on micro-level and macro-level, and their relation with values. The social norms are dynamic in our normative framework. In other words, norms might undergo changes due to changes in the environment including change in the group members, economy, and ecology.

In this paper, we start with some background information and introduce the concept of values as we use it (Sect. 3), and how they relate to social norms (Sect. 4). We introduce the framework (Sect. 4). Then, we discuss alternative representations and dynamics of norms in a normative decision model, and how our framework covers the dynamics of norms (Sect. 5). We summarize the paper in Sect. 6.

2   Related Work

The first question that need to be answered to make a normative framework is: what is the definition of social norms.

Bicchieri defines norms as: "the language a society speaks, the embodiment of its values and collective desires". She specifies norms as behavioral rules that will be triggered in certain social roles or situations [3]. Interesting enough she also mentions that norms are embodiments of values. This is in line with Schwartz, who also argues that specific norms for concrete situations are connected to a set of abstract values [16]. Thus when we use norms we should also model the values from which they are the embodiment. Somehow this aspect is hardly ever used, but we will show its importance in this paper. Bicchieri also mentions that sociologists have not agreed upon a common definition [6].

However, Gibbs discusses different viewpoints of sociologists on social norms [9]. We used his discussion, to extract the points that his discussion emphasized and we cover them in our framework. According to his discussion: norms are agreements of group members; norms regulate behaviour; norms are group expectations in certain circumstances about what should and what should not be done; norms are based on cultural values; norms are abstract patterns of behaviour; and norms are alternative ways to achieve goals.

These points together will cause dynamics of norms in a group. As norms are agreements of the members, these agreements can change if the members change their mind. So, we want our normative framework to have the possibility of covering emerging norms, changing norms, and preserving norms.

Of course we are not the first ones to describe normative frameworks. Some groundwork was done in [2,4,8,18]. Neumann compared some architectures that covers social norms [14].

EMIL-A-1 [12] is a normative architecture based on the EMIL-A architecture which has an explicit norm emergence possibility. However, in this framework there is no connection with values yet. Villatoro introduces a normative architecture that includes sanctions and punishments to increase cooperation in social systems [18]. He mentions that norm emergence and making a self-policy system can be achieved by means of different punishment technologies. However, he mentions that social norms are social cues that guide behaviour even in the absence of explicit punishment systems. From this we take that our framework should not exclusively rely on a punishment system. Most norm abidance comes from the wish to group conformance. Thus, indirectly the group determines the abidance of the norm. We will incorporate this element by letting agents abide by a norm dependent on the visibility of the norm. It does not mean that punishment does not play a role, but rather that it is not the main driver of norm emergence and norm compliance.

In our framework, we define norms as social behavior that might involve punishment or not. In other words, some norms will be followed because people need to satisfy their conformity value[1] and be a good member of their group [7].

As said above, values are the main source of norms as values are "ideals worth pursuing" [7]. Therefore, values can be seen as one of the main ultimate motives of deliberated actions. Norms and values are evaluation scales. However, norms are more concrete embodiments of values. Norms refer to certain behavioral choices in particular contexts; values are criteria to prioritize particular types of actions and situations [13]. For example, a person who highly values unisersalism would like to give away some money for altruistic reasons. However, there might be some social norms that determine how much to donate, when to donate, etc.

As the basis of our framework we use the value system as developed by Schwartz. Schwartz represents a universal theory on value system that is widely known and accepted by researchers [1,17]. We will explain this value system in

---

[1] Conformity is one of 10 abstract values that Schwartz presents in [17]. Conformity drives obedience to rules and social expectations or norms.

more detail in the next section (Sect. 3). Also, we will explain our previous work on representing a value framework based on Schwartz's value theory in Sect. 3.

Fig. 1. Schwartz value circle, categorization and dynamicity of abstract personal values [17]

3 Summary of the Value Framework

Our norm framework is based on our previous work on the value framework [10]. In this section, we briefly review the value framework[2] and discuss how this framework is used as a basis for our norm framework.

Considering Schwartz's value circle, we introduce a framework for decision making based on (personal) values. Schwartz introduces 10 abstract values that are supposed to be universal (Fig. 1). However, the importance and priorities of the values differ. The importance of a value is a degree that shows the salience of a value in a certain situation and time. A value like universalism is less important after just having spend a day doing community work. At that time it might be allowed to relax and enjoy some nice dinner with friends. The priorities between values indicate a base preference between the values. I.e. whether universalism is more important than conservatism in cases where both values are salient for choosing a course of action. Using the visualization of the Schwartz value circle, there are some relations between the priorities of these values. The closer to each other the values are in the circle, the closer is their priority [17].

Similar to the Schwartz circle, in our framework each value has a degree of importance. We defined mathematical equations that maintain the circular relation of the importance of values. To reflect the heterogeneity of agents, agents can have different value importances. In other words, they can assign different degrees of importance to their abstract values. Therefore, two agents with different importance distributions might take different decisions under the same external condition.

In our value framework [10] agents make a deliberate value-based decision. We operationalised the framework using an agent-based model (ABM). For the

---

[2] For further details and implemented version of the framework see [10].

ABM we defined value trees to connect Schwartz abstract values to actions. The root of these trees are the Schwartz abstract values and the leaves of the trees are actions that agents can perform. Nodes that are closer to the leaves are more concrete. Fig. 2 depicts a possible tree for donation in a simulation based on our value framework. In these trees, if an agent performs an action, he will sweep the related value tree up to the root. Then, the assigned water tank to the root will be filled.

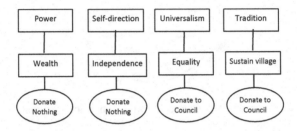

Fig. 2. Sample value trees related to donation action (more examples in [10])

We use water tank model to represent value satisfaction and thus salience of values. We assigned one water tank to each value tree. Each water tank has a threshold level (which is the importance of its value) and its water drains over time. Every time that an action is taken, some water will be poured into the related water tank. Each agent decides what to do based on the difference between water level and threshold of his water tanks. A positive difference means that the value is satisfied; consequently, a negative difference means that the agent did not satisfy the value enough times.

In the next section we will extend this framework with norms. The norms are placed in between the values and the actions. Thus norms can be seen as concrete rules for deciding on actions that will promote a certain value. Thus, instead of having to reason with whole value trees we can use the norms as concrete representations of them. However, by placing the norms in the context of the value trees the agent can also reason about violating a norm in a concrete case, of adopting a norm or adapting it and even abrogating it.

4   The Norm Framework

In this section, we introduce a norm framework for building normative agent-based models and agent-based simulations. In this framework, agents deliberate based on their individual values and the social norms of the groups they are part of. Social norms are formed based on individual values. Agents participate in the dynamics of social norms by following, violating, or even by performing actions that slightly deviate from social norms, thus making social norms dynamic in this framework. In other words, norms might undergo changes due to any change in the environment including group structure, economy, and ecology. On the other hand, because they are tied to values, these changes are also opposed, constrained and directed in a controlled manner. We make use of a preliminary simulation in Sect. 5 to show how these norm dynamics can have profound influences on the behavior of the agents, as well as the structure and behavior of groups.

4.1 Norm Definition

As mentioned earlier, we use the following aspects of norms as used by Gibbs [9] as a basis for the model of social norms in our framework:

1. norms are agreements of group members,
2. norms regulate behaviour,
3. norms are group expectations in certain circumstances about what should and what should not be done,
4. norms are based on values,
5. norms are abstract patterns of behaviour, and
6. norms are alternative ways to achieve goals.

The above points do not mention sanctions explicitly. We follow Gibbs and Bicchieri who mentions that social norms may or may not be supported by sanctions [3]. Thus we do not take sanctions as the main drivers of norm emergence and compliance and they are not part of our core norm model, although they can be added to it to strengthen the effect of norms in certain contexts.

Expanding on point 4 (norms are based on values), provided by Gibbs, we use Bicchieri's research on social norms to connect norms and values. She mentions that norms are embodiments of values [3]. This point of view is supported by other research that illustrates that norms are connected to a set of abstract values with the *aim* of achieving those values [7,16].

Bardi and Schwartz believe that values do not play a role in making behavioral choices directly and consciously for most people. However, people act mostly according to their value system, which is mostly unconscious [1]. In other words, most people have a certain value system, but they do not refer to it for every single decision. Our interpretation of their work is that a person should live a normal life even without deliberating about all his actions through his values. This can be realized by assuming that social norms cover most of the actions that are needed for interactions with other people in daily life.

4.2 Norm Type, Structure and Relation to Values

Considering the arguments in the previous section, we explain how we formulate social norms and how we formulate norms as embodiments of values. We formulate social norms as actions that agents consider to do or not to do in certain conditions.

Therefore, we define a norm n as follows: $n = <v, c, t, a, pe, ne>$ in which n as a social norm guides the agents to satisfy value v by performing action a, under condition c. Depending on the norm type t the agent might get positive consequence pe by following n, get a punishment ne by violating n, or there is no positive social consequence nor any negative social consequence by following or violating n.

Taking the provided definition of social norms, we see that norms are not a necessary completion of values but rather norms and values are complementary. A norm is an edge in the value tree that connects two nodes of the tree whose distance is at least 2. It means that there is a path between these two nodes with length of at least 2. If one of the nodes is an action (leaf of the value tree), the norm is a specific norm; otherwise, it is an abstract norm. Thus the norm can be seen as a shortcut for a value. Reasoning from an action upwards an agent can stop at a node where a norm is connected. Following the norm guarantees promoting the value. Thus if most actions are connected with concrete norms to the value tree above, very little (expensive) reasoning about values has to be done. However, this construction also allows the comparison of two norms by checking which values they promote and which of those values has higher priority and importance. This allows for reasoning about violation of a norm in case norms are inconsistent in specific situations or in case another value is more important than the value promoted by the norm. E.g. speeding in the highway in order to be in time for dinner.

The importance of following a norm differs depending on the importance degree of its supported values and the Norm type. Therefore, consequences of violating and following norms differ. We consider four types of norms: should follow (to represents soft social norms), have to follow (to represents strict social norms), and must follow (to represents laws).

Also, personal characteristics of people play a role on how much they might consider social norms in their decisions, especially if the social norms are in conflict with their personal values. For example, if a person values universalism a lot, he will internalize "donating to public benefits" norm as such a norm serves universalism value. Internalizing a norm raises the probability of considering it in decisions.

4.3   Decision Making

To recognize a normative behavior, an agent considers what most people do [3]. This is what Cialdini et al. define as descriptive norms [5]. However, agents consider the social standing of the person who is performing an action, $S(a)$. $S(a)$ represents the social status of agent a. If an agent has a good social standing, other agents consider his actions with a higher probability.

In our framework, each agent makes a decision about what action to perform considering their personal values and social norms. Each agent has its own value trees. These value trees are not necessarily complete from root to very concrete leaves. In other words, some of the agents might not have value trees explicitly. Either an agent has complete value trees or not, they have those shortcuts that they adopt from the society. Those shortcuts are norms. Norms can cover primary needs of people so that they do not need to reason upon their values to make a decision. Therefore, the agents that have complete value trees explicitly are the ones representing deep thinking people in the real world. In other words, these agents can deliberate about their actions explicitly.

Each agent can be a member of several groups. Therefore, each agent has a list of norms that he adopts from his groups. Such a list is dynamic for two reasons. First, social norms are not explicitly available, but rather individuals have their own understanding of norms. Second, norms are influenced by the environment. In other words, any change in the environment including changes in group members, economic situation, and ecological situation might lead to changes in the social norm. If changing the group members alters the collective values of the group, the group norm will change slightly; as the norms are connected to values. If there is any change in ecology or economy that makes following a norm not viable, a norm might abrogate slowly. For example, assume that there is a norm on donation in a community because people value equality a lot. If many new people who are self-oriented join the society, they can slightly change the norm to donate less frequently, or donate less. Or assume that economic inflation happens and people cannot earn enough money. The donation norm may change to alternative actions such as sharing food, donating cloth, etc.

We assume that each group has its own social norms. Each group might have a different norm on how to do one certain action. It should be noted that we do not consider explicit representations for norms. We do not consider a group as a central element that control and keep norms. But rather, agents perceive norms of a group by monitoring the behaviour of its members over time. To consider group membership and norms, each agent has a list $<N, g>$ in which N is a set of social norms that the agent assigns to group g.

To give an example of group norms, assume "turning trash into treasure to save the environment" as a norm that is serving the universalism value. Assume an agent is working in a company. His colleagues have the norm of "separating plastic bottle caps to donate to charity". The same agent is living in a neighborhood with a norm of "separating glass waste color-wise". Both norms serve universalism value, however they are valid in different contexts.

Each agent considers social norms in his decisions depending on how many times he observed a norm n has been followed by his group mates in group g. An agent will increase the probability of following n, if he observes n has been repeated over time regularly. Normative action of a group g for an agent a_i is a weighted average action of all other agents a_j, where $i \neq j$ and a_j is member of g:

$$n = \frac{\sum_{a_i, a_i \neq a_j}^{a_i \in g} S(a_i) * (\text{performed action by } a_i)}{\sum_{a_i, a_i \neq a_j}^{a_i \in g} S(a_i)},$$

where, $S(a_i)$ is social standing of agent a_i.

So, each agent needs to keep how many times a norm is repeated. A norm has a chance of abrogation if agents stop following it for long enough time. Therefore, we need to keep a variable showing how many time steps a norm has not been repeated. So, each agent keeps a norm repetition as a set of $<n, r, nr>$ that shows norm n has been fulfilled r times and not been used nr times.

As mentioned earlier, an agent regards several factors to make a decision including personal preference, norms, motivations, culture, etc. In this paper, we consider norms and personal values as two factors that effectively regulate behavioral choices. An agent a_j considers both its personal preference and social norm of group g to make a decision in that group. Therefore, we formulate the normative decision according to the following equation:

$$decision = P_n(t) * n(a_j) + (1 - P_n(t)) * \text{personal preference}.$$

Where $n(a_j)$ is norm n that agent a_j considers in his decision. $P_n(t)$ is a probability function that depends on the history of norm n till time t. More explanation on $P_n(t)$ is provided in the Sect. 4.4.

4.4   Norm Life Cycle

In this framework, we consider four phases for a norm, observation, adoption, internalization, and abrogation. Therefore, we define a function $P_n(t)$ (probability of following a norm n) for each agent as follows:

$$P_n(t) = \begin{cases} F_{observe}(t) & \text{if } t \in \text{observation phase} \\ F_{adopt}(t) & \text{if } t \in \text{adoption phase} \\ F_{internal}(t) & \text{if } t \in \text{internalization phase} \\ F_{abrogate}(t) & \text{if } t \in [0, nr] \end{cases}$$

Functions $F_{observe}(t)$, $F_{adopt}(t)$, $F_{internal}(t)$, and $F_{abrogate}(t)$ determine P_n when norm n is in observation, adoption, internalization, and abrogating phase respectively. The repetition times to enter to a new phase of a norm are relative and can be changed based on the particular domain. Despite the numbers assigned to norm phases, the agent increases r by 1 if he observes that most of his neighbors performed accordingly. Otherwise, he resets r and increases nr by 1. In the latter case, the agent will create a new potential norm for an action a. If a starts repeating he will update r; otherwise, he will remove the created norm. Also, when nr reaches the maximum time, the agent will remove the norm as well.

In order to make decisions on norms that might be in different phases of the life cycle we need to have the possibility of considering external and internal norms in our framework. By external norms we mean behaviors that an agent expresses/shows to public. Internal norms are the ones that are compatible with the personal values of an agent and he would like to follow whenever possible. Internal norms can be different from what other people can externally see. For example, an ungenerous person does not want to donate anything (internal norm), but will donate a small amount in order to keep up appearance of following the group norm of donating (external norm).

In the current simulation, the internal norm is represented by using a weighted sum of the values and the external norm in order to decide on a behavior. Thus an internal norm is kept implicit and not managed separately. However, in our framework, internalized norms are the norms that the agent will follow even after leaving a group. Those are the norms that has been repeated enough and are in line with the values of an agent. Therefore, internalized norms are stored as $<N, g>$, where $g = NULL$.

5   Discussion

This section illustrates one of the possible simulations that we developed based on the introduced norm framework. Using this simulation, we discuss some of the interesting simulation examples that explain the importance of a) value-based norms, b) norm dynamics and norm stability; and c) allowing for dynamic groups (agents can enter and leave groups).

We explain how our norm framework helps exploring our questions: how personal values of group members influence social norm of a group, how values make social norms more robust against small changes, how values cause the emergence of a new norm, how values guide the changes of existing norms, and how the social norm influences the individual behaviour of the members.

Simulation Settings. We implemented a community in which we study behavior related to contributions to public good in the form of donations. The amount of donation is normative. So, there are norms going around on the normative amount of donation. Personal preference of the donation amount is connected to values, but it also serves the normative amount of the group which is served by group adherence.

Agents are heterogeneous in their values and organize into different groups. Agents considers social status of all of his group-mates are equal ($S(a_i) = 1$). Agents cannot choose some groups (family), and they can choose some groups(neighbors, colleagues, etc.). An agent can also belong to more than one group at a time.

One possible setting of $P_n(t)$ that we used for our simulation is:

$$P_n(t) = \begin{cases} \alpha_1 * t & \text{if } 0 < t < 5 \\ e(t - 10.35708268) - 0.00028536; & \text{if } 5 <= t < 10 \\ 1 - 1/t^0.5 & \text{if } 10 <= t < 20 \\ 1/(1 + 0.0078 * 0.5^{(25-t')}) & \text{if } t' >= 10 \end{cases}$$

in which t' is number of times that norm n has stopped repeating. According to this setting, the probability of following a norm does not increase mush as the agent is still not sure about the norm. However, P_n increases exponentially during adoption phase. As mentioned prior, a norm enters to the internalization phase if it has been repeated enough by other agents and if it is compatible with the personal value of an agent. Therefore, an internalized norm has a higher chance of being followed by an agents.

Assume group g_1 has 4 members, agents a_1, a_2, a_3, a_4, who value power a lot (with the importance of 80%). Therefore, norm of the group emerged as n_1 =< power, "having more than enough money", should follow, donate 5%–10%, raise social status, null >. Consider agents a_5, a_6, a_7, a_8 highly value universalism (with the importance of 80%) and they used to donate about 50% on average (either because of their internalized norm or because of their other groups)

Scenario 1. Robustness of Norms. Our simulation shows if a_5 joins g_1, he starts adopting norm n_1. He donates 10% mostly (according to external norm of the group). Agent g_5 seldom deviates from norm n_1 to keep his social image. But, he rarely donates 50% (according to his internalized norm) to satisfy his universalism value. However, his attitude does not change the norm. After he start adopting the norm, a_6 joins the group. The same will happen to a_6 and any other agents that joins the group with the same pattern. In this scenario, norm is stabled over time. Even though the social norm is different from the internalized norm for $a_5..a_8$.

An exceptional case can lead to changing the group norm. If a new universalist agent a_i join the group at time tick t. Assume agents $a_5..a_8$ join the group at time tick $t+1$ to $t+4$ respectively and donate 50%. Agent a_i observes that the average donation is 15%. With our simulation setting that observation time is 5 time ticks, he will start adopting norm of "donate about 15%" as the norm of g_1. If more agents similar to a_i join the group and the same story happens to them, n_1 will deviate a bit from its original amount.

Scenario 2. Changing of Norms. We ran the simulation to check what will happen if a lot of new members enter a group at the same time. We let agents $a_5..a_8$ joins group g_1 together at time tick t. During the observation phase, agents $a_5..a_8$ donate 50% according to their internalized norm. Therefore, they observe that donation amount is about 27% on average. So, they adopt "donating about 27%" as the norm of g_1. However, the other agents $a_1..a_4$ start realizing that normal donation is changing from time tick $t+1$. When they observe the new donation amount for more than 10 time ticks (which is the minimum time to abrogate a norm in our simulation setting), they abrogate their perceived norm and start observing the group behaviour again. From time $t+5$ onward, the new members mostly donate the normative of 27%. From time $t+6$, the new members will see that the average amount is different from what they start adopting (which is about 12% now). Therefore, they do not adopt normative amount 27%, but rather start observing whether 12% is a norm till time tick $t+10$. Continuing this run, the normative donation amount of the group converges to 27%. The convergence happens because agents ignore some of the random deviation from norm.

The above simulation scenarios shows partly how individual values guide emergence, robustness, and changes of social norms. In these two scenarios, the same agents joined a group with different patterns. If new agents join gradually, they can hardly change values' balance of the group. Therefore, norm the group stays stable. But, if new agents join altogether a the same time, they can change existing norm if it is against their values.

6 Conclusion

In this paper, we introduce a norm framework. Such a framework considers social norms as non-static social elements. In our framework, norm dynamics arise from dynamic environments. Such a framework is not completely new in the field of social simulation. However, we connect norms to personal values and consider norms as embodiments of personal values. This connection makes the norms robust against small dynamics in the environment. In addition, it is more realistic as there is no need to have a central element to monitor and keep social norms. But rather, social norms are distributed between agents as their perception of social norms. We discuss how such as a framework can express the way values guide norms (emergence, changing, abrogation, and internalization). We explained it using a preliminary simulation scenarios.

References

1. Bardi, A., Schwartz, S.H.: Values and behavior: strength and structure of relations. Pers. Soc. Psychol. Bull. **29**(10), 1207–1220 (2003)
2. Beheshti, R.: Modeling social norms in real-world agent-based simulations. Ph.D. thesis, University of Central Florida (2015)
3. Bicchieri, C.: The Grammar of Society: the Nature and Dynamics of Social Norms, vol. 1. Cambridge University Press, Cambridge (2006)
4. Broersen, J., Dastani, M., Hulstijn, J., van der Torre, L.: Goal generation in the BOID architecture. Cogn. Sci. Q. **2**(3–4), 428–447 (2002)
5. Cialdini, R.B., Kallgren, C.A., Reno, R.R.: A focus theory of normative conduct: a theoretical refinement and reevaluation of the role of norms in human behavior. Adv. Exp. Soc. Psychol. **24**, 201–234 (1991)
6. Conte, R., Andrighetto, G., Campenni, M.: Minding Norms: Mechanisms and Dynamics of Social Order in Agent Societies. Oxford University Press, Oxford (2014)
7. Dechesne, F., Di Tosto, G., Dignum, V., Dignum, F.: No smoking here: values, norms and culture in multi-agent systems. Artif. Intell. Law **21**(1), 79–107 (2013)
8. Dignum, F., Dignum, V., Prada, R., Jonker, C.M.: A conceptual architecture for social deliberation in multi-agent organizations. Multiagent Grid Syst. **11**(3), 147–166 (2015)
9. Gibbs, J.P.: Norms: the problem of definition and classification. Am. J. Sociol. **70**(5), 586–594 (1965)
10. Heidari, S., Jensen, M., Dignum, F.: Simulation with values. In: Social Simulation Conference (2018)
11. Hofstede, G.J.: GRASP agents: social first, intelligent later. AI Soc. J. Hum. Mach. Intell. **34**(3), 535–543 (2017)

12. López, F.L.y., Luck, M., d'Inverno, M.: A normative framework for agent-based systems. Comput. Math. Organ. Theory **12**(2), 227–250 (2006)

13. Marini, M.M.: Social values and norms (2018). https://www.encyclopedia.com/social-sciences/encyclopedias-almanacs-transcripts-and-maps/social-values-and-norms

14. Neumann, M.: The cognitive legacy of norm simulation. Artif. Intell. Law **20**(4), 339–357 (2012)

15. Pastrav, C., Dignum, F.: Norms in social simulation: balancing between realism and scalability. In: Verhagen, H., Borit, M., Bravo, G., Wijermans, N. (eds.) Advances in Social Simulation. SPC, pp. 329–342. Springer, Cham (2020). https://doi.org/10.1007/978-3-030-34127-5_32

16. Schwartz, S.H.: Normative influences on altruism. Adv. Exp. Soc. Psychol. **10**, 221–279 (1977)

17. Schwartz, S.H.: Universals in the content and structure of values: theoretical advances and empirical tests in 20 countries. In: Advances in Experimental Social Psychology, vol. 25, pp. 1–65. Academic Press (1992)

18. Villatoro, D.: Social norms for self-policing multi-agent systems and virtual societies, Ph.D. thesis, Universitat Autònoma de Barcelona (2011)

Author Index

Printed in the United States
By Bookmasters